Sweet
Crochet Frie

Amigurumi Creations from Khuc Cay

HOANG THI NGOC ANH

Tuva

Titou The Tiger
102

Toto Racoon
108

Vivi
The Bunny
114

Willis The Goat
122

CONTENTS

PROJECTS

Tuva Publishing
www.tuvapublishing.com

Address Merkez Mah. Cavusbasi Cad. No71
Cekmekoy - Istanbul 34782 / Turkey
Tel +9 0216 642 62 62

Sweet Crochet Friends

First Print 2019 / September

All Global Copyrights Belong To
Tuva Tekstil ve Yayıncılık Ltd.

Content Crochet

Editor in Chief Ayhan DEMİRPEHLİVAN
Project Editor Kader DEMİRPEHLİVAN
Author HOANG Thi Ngoc Anh
Technical Editors Leyla ARAS, Büşra ESER
Graphic Designers Ömer ALP, Abdullah BAYRAKÇI, Zilal ÖNEL
Photography Tuva Publishing, HOANG Thi Ngoc Anh
Illustrations HOANG Thi Ngoc Anh
Crochet Tech Editor Wendi CUSINS

ISBN 978-605-9192-70-5

Thank you  for supporting this book with your yarn.

 TuvaYayincilik TuvaPublishing
 TuvaYayincilik TuvaPublishing

Introduction

My crochet journey began in December 2017, when I made a little bunny hat for my daughter. Before that, for twenty-five years, I did not know what a crochet hook was, nor what it was used for. But thanks to modern technology and the internet, I learnt the elements of crochet – holding the hook and yarn and working basic crochet stitches – all from watching YouTube videos. I was so proud of myself!

My mother, a very traditional Vietnamese woman, loved cooking and making things using various handcrafts. Growing up, I remember wearing beautiful clothes that she had either sewn or knitted for us. She taught my sisters and me how to make doll's clothes, and we played with our dolls every day. These childhood memories have influenced me greatly.

After graduating from university in Economics, I had no idea what I wanted to do. At that time, my passion was drawing (another self-taught skill) and I opened an Instagram account to share my pictures. There was a lot of interest in them, and so I started an online shop, selling my illustrations.

Soon after I finished making the crocheted bunny hat, I discovered Amigurumi and stuffed crocheted toys. I fell in love with this technique and have not looked back. Everything fell into place for me! My imagination now comes to life as I design and create these cute toys myself!

Writing my own crochet book is a dream come true. It has been an incredible experience putting everything together – from the initial sketches of the characters, through to the final embellishments on the finished toys. Not to mention the step-by-step photographs needed for each design.

I might not have many years of experience in crocheting, but I hope you will find something fresh and new in this book. I believe there are no strict rules for stitches or techniques (or any crochet-related things, in fact), and each toy you make, will have your own special signature. Even if you make a little mistake, that imperfection will make your toy perfectly unique. As long as you are doing this with love, you will see amazing results, the beautiful soul from your hands.

Throughout the book, not only will you find the instructions for making the toys, but also some of my tips and tricks, some cute little histories, and even some of my illustrations. Grab your hooks and some yarn and come and join me.
Let's have some fun together, crocheting these sweet little friends.

Hoang Thi Ngoc Anh - aka 'Khuc Cay'

Materials & Tools

Crochet & Amigurumi Basics

Crochet Terminology

As a beginner, you might find reading crochet patterns very confusing. Designers and/or publishers all use different styles and terminology when it comes to writing patterns. Below you will find information about the abbreviations and symbols used in this book, which uses US crochet terminology.

1. Basic Conversion Chart

US	UK
slip stitch (sl st)	slip stitch (sl st)
chain (ch)	chain (ch)
single crochet (sc)	double crochet (dc)
double crochet (dc)	treble crochet (tr)
half-double crochet (hdc)	half treble (htr)
treble (triple) crochet (tr)	double treble (dtr)

2. Abbreviations of the Basic Stitches

st/sts	stitch/stitches
ch	chain stitch
sl st	slip stitch
sc	single crochet stitch
hdc	half-double crochet stitch
dc	double crochet stitch
tr	treble (or triple) crochet stitch

3. Concise Action Terms

dec	Decrease (reduce by one or more stitches)
inc	Increase (add one or more stitches)
join	1) To finish a round, usually with a slip stitch to the first stitch. 2) To introduce a new color.
turn	Turn your crochet piece to work back in the next row/round.
BLO	back loops only
FLO	front loops only

4. Standard Symbols Used in Patterns

[ ]	Work instructions within brackets as many times as directed.
( )	1- Work instructions within parentheses all in the same stitch or space. 2- Indicates the stitch count at the end of the row/round.
*	Repeat the instructions following the single (or double) asterisk as directed.
......	Repeat instructions between two single asterisks as many times as directed or repeat at specified locations.

5. Skill Level Chart

Symbol	Skill Level	Definition
♥	Easy	Uses basic stitches, with simple color changes. Simple shaping and finishing.
♥♥	Intermediate	Uses a variety of stitches and techniques. Mid-level shaping and finishing.
♥♥♥	Advanced	Uses intricate stitch patterns and multi-colored techniques. Detailed shaping and refined finishing.

6. Reading Crochet Patterns

Here are some explanations of how to follow instructions:

Example 1

Round 4: [Sc in each of next 2 sts, inc in next st] 6 times. (24 sc)

To work round 4, you need to repeat the instructions found between the square brackets – sc in each of next 2 sts, inc in next st – six times. You start by working a single crochet in each of the next 2 stitches and then work 2 single crochets into the next stitch (increase made). This then gets repeated for another five times. At the end of the round, you can check the stitch count as you should now have 24 single crochets.

Example 2

Rounds 10-16: (7 Rounds) Sc in each st around. (35 sc)

This reads that the rounds from Round 10 to Round 16 will all have the same instructions. It also notifies you that there are seven rounds where this happens. The instruction is to work a single crochet in each stitch around for each round. The stitch count at the end of each of the seven rounds should be 35 single crochets.

Example 3

Round 2: Ch 2, (**bob**, hdc) in each st around; join with sl st to first bobble. (6 bobble sts & 6 hdc)

You start the round by making two chains (to bring the row up to the height of the stitches). Then, in each stitch around, you will work both a bobble stitch and a half-double crochet stitch all in the same stitch. At the end of the round, you will join the round by making a slip stitch into the first bobble stitch you made (after the ch-2). The stitch count for this round does not include the ch-2 as it is not counted as a stitch.

Note: The emboldened "bob" means that this is the first time this stitch is used in the pattern and you need to refer to the stitch definition for it.

Materials & Tools

YARN

There are many choices of yarn you can use for making toys, depending on your preference. The only thing worth considering, is that the yarn should not be elastic and stretch out of shape when stuffing is added.

Most of the time, I use a cotton (or cotton blend) yarn for my toys. It gives their surface a smooth and clean texture, which I like. Sometimes I use Merino wool for a different texture, especially on clothes or accessories. My suggestion is to experiment with several kinds of yarn until you find the one which works for you.

Throughout this book, the following Scheepjes Yarns are used. Except where a pattern calls for "small amounts", you will need at least a half to a full ball of each color listed.

③ LIGHT *Scheepjes* Softfun

Fiber Content 60% Cotton & 40% Acrylic
Yarn Weight Light Weight / DK
Ball Weight 1¾ oz; 50 gram
Length 153 yard; 140 meter

③ LIGHT *Scheepjes* Softfun Denim

Fiber Content 60% Cotton & 40% Acrylic
Yarn Weight Light Weight / DK
Ball Weight 1¾ oz; 50 gram
Length 153 yard; 140 meter

③ LIGHT *Scheepjes* Merino Soft

Fiber Content 50% Wool Superwash Merino, 25% Microfiber & 25% Acrylic
Yarn Weight Light Weight / DK
Ball Weight 1¾ oz; 50 gram
Length 115 yard; 105 meter

② FINE *Scheepjes* Stone Washed

Fiber Content 78% Cotton & 22% Acrylic
Yarn Weight Fine / Sport Weight
Ball Weight 1¾ oz; 50 gram
Length 142 yard; 130 meter

① SUPER FINE *Scheepjes* Catona

Fiber Content 100% Mercerized Cotton
Yarn Weight Super Fine / Fingering Weight
Ball Weight 1¾ oz; 50 gram
Length 137 yard; 125 meter

Ball Weight ⅞ oz; 25 gram
Length 68 yard; 62.5 meter

Ball Weight ⅜ oz; 10 gram
Length 27 yard; 25 meter

① SUPER FINE *Scheepjes* Catona Denim

Fiber Content 100% Cotton
Yarn Weight Super Fine / Fingering Weight
Ball Weight 1¾ oz; 50 gram
Length 137 yard; 125 meter

Embroidery Thread

A dark-colored embroidery thread can be used to create eyes, instead of using safety eyes. Using different colored threads, you can also add embroidery to embellish your toys. I use Scheepjes Maxi Sweet Treat as my embroidery thread of choice.

⓪ LACE *Scheepjes* Maxi Sweet Treat

Fiber Content 100% Mercerized Cotton
Yarn Weight Lace Weight
Ball Weight ⅞ oz; 25 gram
Length 153 yard; 140 meter

HOOK

When I first started crocheting, I bought a basic steel hook. It worked fine, but did not feel comfortable in my hand. I then discovered the Clover brand of hooks, and I love them.

When making toys, choose a hook which is a size or two smaller than what is recommended for the yarn.

My favorite hook for most of the Sport or DK weight yarns is the 2.50mm.

Hook Size Conversion Table

Metric	U.S	UK/Canada
2.00 mm	-	14
2.25 mm	B-1	13
2.50 mm	-	12
2.75 mm	C-2	-
3.00 mm	-	11
3.125 mm	D	-
3.25 mm	D-3	10
3.50 mm	E-4	9
3.75 mm	F-5	-
4.00 mm	G-6	8
4.25 mm	G	-
4.50 mm	#7	7
5.00 mm	H-8	6
5.25 mm	I	-
5.50 mm	I-9	5
6.00 mm	J-10	4
6.50 mm	K-10 ½	3

NEEDLES

1- Yarn Needle

The yarn (or tapestry) needle is an essential tool. Besides using it for weaving in yarn ends and sewing the different crochet pieces together, it is also used for closing holes and invisible joining. Make sure the eye of the needle is large enough for the yarn you're using. A blunt-tipped needle is preferable (as it will not split the yarn), but you can also use a bent-tipped needle if you like. For toy-making, I find that metal tapestry needles work a lot better than the plastic ones.

2- Embroidery Needle

An embroidery needle can be identified as having a sharp tip and an eye large enough to accommodate the embroidery thread.

3- Needle & Thread

Having sewing needles and thread in your crochet kit, is an advantage. They are needed for sewing on buttons and making small fabric accessories. Choose straight metal needles and a selection of various thread colors.

STITCH MARKER

Most of the crocheted parts of the toys are worked in a spiral. Using a stitch marker, placed in the last stitch of a round, helps keep track of the round number you are working on, as well as making it easier to count the stitches for that round. There are various kinds of stitch markers you can use. Some are made of plastic, others are metallic. Lockable stitch markers are very popular. You can also use safety pins or bobby pins. Using a separate strand of yarn, in a different color, can also mark the ends of rounds. (And here's my confession... I rarely use a stitch marker when making toys! I just count the stitches in my head as I go. However, when making the toys for this book, I did use them, as you can see from the photos).

SAFETY EYES

Safety eyes come in a variety of sizes and colors. Each eye is made up of two parts – the "eye", which has a ribbed shaft, and a washer, which gets secured onto the shaft. I recommend using good quality products, as I have heard stories where the washer came loose and the eye fell off. (Please read the General Safety Warning & Tips).

Fitting Safety Eyes

Choose and mark the position for the eyes on the front of the head. From the right side of the fabric, insert the shaft of the eye through the gap between the stitches.

The eye is on the outside and the shaft is on the inside of the head. Once you are happy with the each eye's position, attach the washer to the shaft and push it in firmly to lock it.

The eye is now securely fitted.

Note: If you struggle to attach the washer firmly, use a safety eye insertion tool to do the job.

STUFFING

There are many different types of stuffing available, such as polyester, wool, cotton, etc. I use polyester fiberfill for my toys, as it's not difficult to find and is inexpensive. It's easy to use and holds its shape well. The great thing is, it is washable!

Stuffing is an important part of toy-making. To achieve a good final result, do not overstuff your toy, as this can stretch the fabric and the stuffing becomes visible between the stitches.

On the other hand, not adding enough stuffing can make a toy "lumpy-looking". My advice is to add stuffing little by little, comparing your toy with the photograph of the model. Keep adding the stuffing, until the toy looks and feels right.

BLUSHER

I love adding some color to the cheeks of toys - and sometimes also to the inner ears. I use a cosmetic blusher and apply it with a small make-up brush or a cotton bud (Q-Tip). Sometimes I use a pink or orange crayon.

OTHER MATERIALS

Pins - I find the straight pins (with large heads) are very helpful – both for marking positions or for keeping pieces in position before sewing.

Scissors – My pair of scissors is a smallish pair which fits into my crochet hook case. They are sharp enough to cut and trim yarns and threads.

Buttons – I keep a small tin of buttons. They're handy to add as an embellishment to a toy.

Felt, Fabric, & Ribbon – Another tin is used to keep all my fabric scraps and left overs. I never know when I might need something!

General Safety Warning & Tips

When making toys for young children under the age of three years (including babies and pets) please take into account the following precautions.

» Make sure each piece of the toy is firmly and securely sewn together so that they cannot pull apart.

» Avoid attaching adornments to the toy which can be pulled or chewed off and swallowed.

» For facial features (eyes, nose, mouth), you can either embroider them, or crochet small circles or ovals and sew them on securely, or cut out felt shapes and stitch them onto the face.

Use child-friendly products:

» Fuzzy yarns are not a good idea as the lint fibers can be inhaled or swallowed.
» Do not use glass eyes or beads which can break and shatter.
» Refrain from using small beads and buttons (including certain safety eyes) which can be chewed off and either get swallowed or become a choking hazard.
» Choose suitable stuffing which can be encased securely. Avoid using plastic or polystyrene pellets as stuffing.
» Use yarn and materials which can be laundered.

NOTE: If you intend selling your finished products, make sure they comply with your country's Toy Safety regulations.

Laundry Instructions

It is best to wash your toys by hand (if the materials are all washable). Mix up a basin of cool, mild soapy water and immerse your toy into it, gently pressing down to fully saturate the toy. Leave it to soak for about half an hour in the soapy solution. Remove the toy, gently squeezing out the excess water. Discard the soapy water and fill the basin with cool, clean water. Immerse the toy in the clean water to rinse and remove the soap. You might need to change the water a few times.

When clean, squeeze the toy gently to remove excess water. Wrap the toy in thick towels and gently roll the towels to absorb most of the water from the toy. Place the nearly dry toy on clean, dry towels, and leave to dry completely. (Some people prefer washing yarn balls before using them. Follow the same directions for washing and drying, keeping the yarn ball intact).

Hint: When giving a toy as a gift (or selling it), it is wise to include safety warnings and laundry instructions.

General Information for Making Stuffed Toys

1. Working in a Spiral

When making stuffed toys, most of the pieces are worked in a continuous spiral to create the dimensional shapes needed. Working in a spiral means that at the end of a round, you do not join (or close) with a slip stitch into the first stitch of the round. When you get to the end of the round, you start the next round by just working a stitch into the next stitch (which is the first stitch of the previous round).

2. Working in Closed Rounds

Some parts of the toy might need to be made in "joined rounds". This is where, at the end of the round, you join with a slip stitch in the first stitch of the round. The next round starts with a number of chain stitches (based on height of the stitches used), and then you continue working stitches for the next round.

Note: Do not turn at the end of each joined round, unless instructed to do so.

3. Working in Rows

For some of the accessories needed for the toys, you will need to work in rows. Each row starts by turning the piece and working some chain stitches (known as the "turning chain"). The number of chain stitches worked is based on the height of the stitches used.

4. Right / Wrong Side

Right Side

It is important to be able to distinguish between the "right" (front) and "wrong" (back) side of the crocheted fabric.

Wrong Side

When working in a spiral or joined round, the right side of the fabric is always facing you. Working in rows or turned rounds, it will alternate between "right" and "wrong" side.

Single Crochet Rows

Adapting The Designs – How To Make Your Toys Unique

1 - Size: By choosing a different weight yarn, you can make your toys either bigger (using thicker yarn) or smaller (using thinner yarn or thread). Remember to change your hook size too.

2 - Color Choice: This is the easiest way to make your toy unique. Select colors to match décor or personal preference.

3 - Character: Changing the facial features of toys, gives them a whole new character. By adding (or removing) embellishments to the overall toy, can change the whole look of it.

4 - Appliqué Patches: Whether they are crocheted, fabric or felt (or a combination of these), adding appliqué patches to your doll is a great way to make your toys distinctive. They can be facial features, such as eyes, noses, mouths, cheeks, and maybe even ears. You can also make novelty appliqué patches to use as embellishment on the toys.

For example – flowers on a dress, eye-patch for a pirate, overall patch for a farmer. The creativity becomes endless.

5 - Accessories: You can add various decorative accessories to your toy. Colored buttons can be used in a variety of ways to spice things up. Using small ribbons and bows can feminize dolls. Attaching a small bunch of flowers or small basket to a doll's hand, tells a new story.

6 - Embroidery: By adding embroidery stitches to the face, the expression of the toy can change. Whether you use plain embroidery stitches (straight stitch, back stitch, etc.) or fancy ones (satin stitch, French knot, bullion stitch, etc.), your toy will take on a personality of its own. You can also use embroidered cross-stitches on your toys to create a different look.

Whichever way you choose to adapt the design, each toy you make, ends up being a one-of-a-kind creation.

Basic Crochet Stitches

1. Slip Knot

Almost every crochet project starts with a slip knot on the hook. This is not mentioned in any pattern - it is assumed.

To make a slip knot, form a loop with your yarn (the tail end hanging behind your loop); insert the hook through the loop, and pick up the ball end of the yarn. Draw yarn through loop. Keeping loop on hook, gently tug the tail end to tighten the knot. Tugging the ball end tightens the loop.

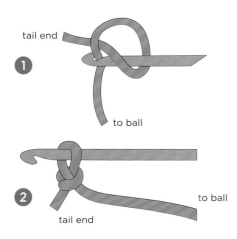

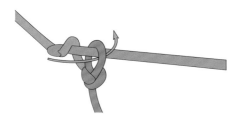

2. Chain Stitch (ch)

The chain stitch is the foundation of most crochet projects. The foundation chain is a series of chain stitches in which you work the first row of stitches.

To make a chain stitch, you start with a slip knot (or loop) on the hook. Yarn over and pull the yarn through the loop on your hook (first chain stitch made). For more chain stitches, repeat: Yarn over, pull through loop on hook.

Hint: Don't pull the stitches too tight, otherwise they will be difficult to work in. When counting chain stitches, do not count the slip knot, nor the loop on the hook. Only count the number of "v"s.

Front of Chain
6 chain stitches

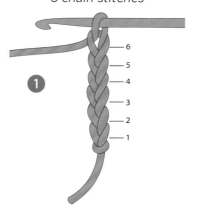

Back of Chain
6 chain stitches

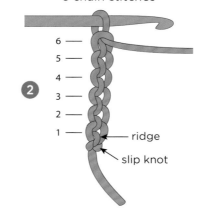

ridge
slip knot

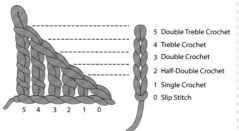

5 Double Treble Crochet
4 Treble Crochet
3 Double Crochet
2 Half-Double Crochet
1 Single Crochet
0 Slip Stitch

3. Slip Stitch (sl st)

Starting with a loop on your hook, insert hook in stitch or space specified and pull up a loop, pulling it through the loop on your hook as well.

The slip stitch is commonly used to attach new yarn and to join rounds.

4. Single Crochet (sc)

Starting with a loop on your hook, insert hook in stitch or space specified and draw up a loop (two loops on hook). Yarn over and pull yarn through both the loops on your hook (first sc made).

The height of a single crochet stitch is one chain high.

When working single crochet stitches into a foundation chain, begin the first single crochet in the second chain from the hook. The skipped chain stitch provides the height of the stitch.
At the beginning of a single crochet row or round, start by making one chain stitch (to get the height) and work the first single crochet stitch into first stitch

Note: The one chain stitch is never counted as a single crochet stitch.

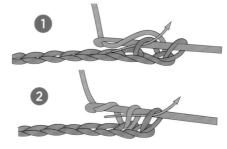

5. Half-Double Crochet (hdc)

Starting with a loop on your hook, yarn over hook before inserting hook in stitch or space specified and draw up a loop (three loops on hook). Yarn over and pull yarn through all three loops (first hdc made).

The height of a half-double crochet stitch is two chains high. When working half-double crochet stitches into a foundation chain, begin the first stitch in the third chain from the hook. The two skipped chains provide the height. When starting a row or round with a half-double crochet stitch, make two chain stitches and work in the first stitch

Note: The two chain stitches are never counted as a half-double stitch.

6. Double Crochet (dc)

Starting with a loop on your hook, yarn over hook before inserting hook in stitch or space specified and draw up a loop (three loops on hook). Yarn over and pull yarn through two loops (two loops remain on hook). Yarn over and pull yarn through remaining two loops on hook (first dc made).

The height of a double crochet stitch is three chains high.

When working double crochet stitches into a foundation chain, begin the first stitch in the fourth chain from the hook.

The three skipped chains count as the first double crochet stitch. When starting a row or round with a double crochet stitch, make three chain stitches (which count as the first double crochet), skip the first stitch (under the chains) and work a double crochet in the next (second) stitch.

On the following row or round, when you work in the 'made' stitch, you will be working in the top chain (3rd chain stitch of the three chains).

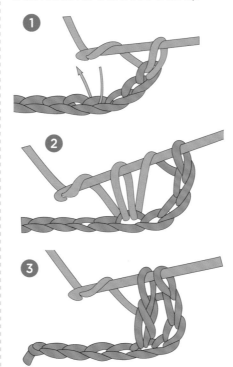

Tip: *When I work double crochet stitches in closed rounds, I start the round with two chain stitches (which do not count as the first stitch), and work the first double crochet of the round into the same stitch as the previous round's join. At the end of the round, join with a slip stitch into the first double crochet you made (skipping the ch-2). By doing it this way, there are no "holes" at the joins.*

7. Treble (or Triple) Crochet (tr)

Starting with a loop on your hook, yarn over hook twice before inserting hook in stitch or space specified and draw up a loop (four loops on hook).

Yarn over and pull yarn through two loops (three loops remain on hook). Again, make a yarn over and pull yarn through two loops (two loops remain on hook). Once more, yarn over and pull through remaining two loops (first tr made).

The height of a treble crochet stitch is four chains high. When working treble crochet stitches into a foundation chain, begin the first stitch in the fifth chain from the hook. The four skipped chains count

as the first treble crochet stitch. When starting a row or round with a treble crochet stitch, make four chain stitches (which count as the first treble crochet), skip the first stitch (under the chains) and work a treble crochet in the next (second) stitch. On the following row or round, when you work in the 'made' stitch, you will be working in the top chain (4th chain stitch of the four chains).

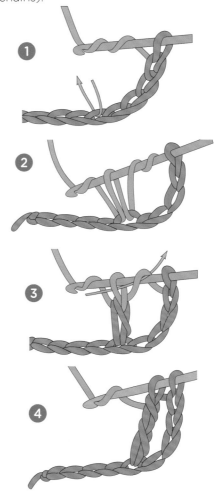

Special Stitches & Techniques Used

Modified Single Crochet

The normal way of doing single crochet creates "V"-shaped stitches. I prefer making the single crochet stitches "X"-shaped.

I find these stitches to be a lot neater when making toys and also prevent the stuffing from showing.

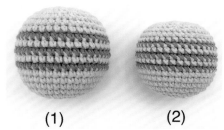

Comparison between normal V-shaped single crochet (1) and X-shaped single crochet (2), using same hook, yarn and pattern.

To do these X-shaped stitches, insert your hook into the next stitch, place the hook in front of the yarn and with the hook facing downwards, grab the yarn and pull through the stitch. (This is known as a "yarn under".) With the two loops on your hook, you complete the stitch as normal – in other words, yarn over and draw through both loops on hook.

Demonstrating Yarn Under Technique

The Difference Between "Yarn Over" And "Yarn Under"

For "yarn over", keep the yarn behind the hook and wrap the yarn over the hook from back to front.

For "yarn under", keep the hook behind the yarn, and wrap the yarn under the hook from front to back.

Single Crochet Decrease (sc-dec)

Tip: *When making toys, I mostly use the invisible decrease as it doesn't leave gaps and gives a neater result.*

a) Normal Decrease

Step 1: Insert hook in next stitch and pull up a loop (2 loops on hook).

Step 2: Insert hook in next stitch and pull up a loop (3 loops on hook).

Step 3: Yarn over, draw through all three loops on hook. Normal decrease made

b) Invisible Decrease

Step 1: Insert hook in the front loop of each of the next 2 stitches.

Step 2: Pull yarn through the two stitch loops on hook (2 loops remain on hook).

Step 3: Yarn over and draw through both loops on hook. Invisible decrease made.

Single Crochet Increase (inc)

Work two single crochet stitches in the same stitch or space specified.

Magic (Adjustable) Ring

1- Form a loop with the yarn, keeping the tail end of the yarn behind the working yarn (the yarn attached to the ball).

2- Insert the hook through the loop (from front to back), and pull the working yarn through the loop (from back to front). Do not tighten up the loop.

3- Using the working yarn, make a chain stitch (to secure the ring). This chain stitch does NOT count as first stitch.

4- Work the required stitches into the ring (over the tail strand). When all the stitches are done, gently tug the tail end to close the ring, before joining the round (if specified). Remember, make sure this tail is firmly secured before weaving in the end.

Note: If you prefer, you can use any type of "ring" to start your project (or start with ch-2, and working the first round in the second chain from hook). The advantage of using the adjustable Magic Ring, is that when it is tightened, it closes the hole completely.

Tip: Secure your Magic Ring after the first few rounds and before you start stuffing.

working yarn

tail end

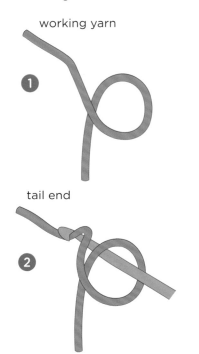

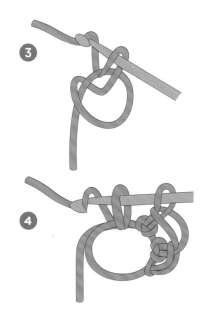

Working Around a Foundation Chain

When you want to start an oval piece rather than a round piece, I use this a lot for making ears but also sometimes for starting a main part of a character.

Start with the required amount of stitches in a chain. Single crochet into the second chain from the hook (if making an oval this will usually also be an increase stitch) and in each chain along. The last chain is where you need to put your increases (this will be indicated on the pattern) as you make the increases you will naturally turn to work up the other side of the foundation chain (this will be the other loop of the foundation chain).

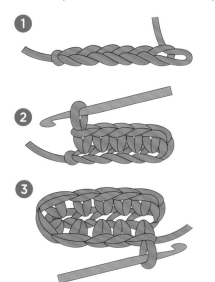

Changing Colors

Always change colors in the final step of the last stitch of the current color:

With two loops of the last stitch remaining on the hook.

Pull new color through the remaining two loops.

Continue following the pattern with the new color.

There are many ways to manage the yarn tail when changing colors. You can use any method that gives you the desired result. In my patterns, I use the following.

a) Stranding Method

When changing to a new color, drop the old color to the inside of the work and then pick it up again when it's needed, creating a strand on the inside. Keep the strands loose enough, so the fabric does not pucker.

Tip: *I use this method only when there are less than 3 stitches between color changes in a stuffed piece (e.g. Body of Rosie Horse), or less than 5 stitches in a non-stuffed part (e.g. Ears of Willis Goat).*

b) Cut and Tie Method

When there are more than 3 to 5 stitches between the color changes, I prefer to cut the old color and then tie the old and new color tails together on the inside of the piece.

Tip: *When changing between dark and light colors, I suggest you weave in all the dark ends into the back of the dark stitches before stuffing, so that the dark color will not be visible through the light-colored stitches.*

c) Stripe Pattern

To give a different appearance to the toys, one can also alternate colors each round. When changing colors, do not cut the yarn. Carry the yarn on the inside of the toy.

Note: Changing colors in a spiral will always be noticeable in a striped pattern.

There are ways to avoid this (refer to the internet). I prefer making the color changes at the back (or to one side) of the toy, so that it is not visible from the front.

Crochet Surface Slip Stitches

These decorative stitches look like embroidered chain stitches. Make a slip knot in the yarn. Insert hook into crocheted fabric from the front (right side) to the back (wrong side) and place the slip knot on hook.

Keeping the yarn at the back, pull up the loop of the slip knot through the fabric to the front, keeping the knot at the back.

*Insert hook in the next spot specified, from front to back.

And pull up a loop through the fabric and through the loop on the hook.

Repeat from * as instructed to make the surface chain.

Front and Back Loops

Every stitch has what looks like "v"s on the top. There are two loops that make up the "v". The front loop is the loop closest to you and the back loop is the loop furthest from you. Generally, we work in both loops – under both the front and back loops. Working in either the front or back loops only, creates a decorative ridge (made up of the unworked loops).

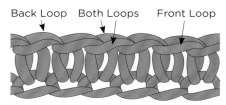

Note: Work all stitches under both loops unless otherwise instructed.

Attach (Join) Yarn

When starting a new strand of yarn, insert the hook in the stitch or space specified and fold the new yarn over the hook.

Pull the yarn through the stitch or space.

Continue with the pattern instructions.

Fasten Off

After the last stitch is made, cut the yarn, leaving a tail.

Pull the tail through the stitch.

If you have to sew the piece later, keep the tail long (about 6" or 15 cm), depending on how many stitches you need to sew).

Weave in Ends

Thread the yarn tail onto a needle. Starting close to where the tail begins, working in the wrong side of the fabric, weave the tail through the back of stitches to hide the yarn.

When done, trim the tail close to the fabric.

For weaving in ends on a stuffed piece, you can secure the yarn close to the piece, insert the needle through the stuffing and out the other side. Repeat this a few times. Cut the yarn close to the surface of the piece.

Invisible (Needle) Join

After fastening off (as described earlier), thread the tail onto a yarn needle. Skip the next stitch, insert the needle under both loops of the following stitch.

Then insert the needle into the back loop of the last stitch made (the same stitch where the tail came through).

Pull the yarn gently so that it looks like a stitch and matches the size of the other stitches.

Secure this stitch and weave in ends.

Close the Remaining Stitches

When you finish a piece, there might be a small hole in the center of the last round of stitches. There are many ways to close this hole, and with experience you will find the method which suits you best.

This is how I do it:
After fastening off, thread the yarn tail onto a needle. Working in the last round of stitches, insert the needle (from outside to inside) through the front loops only of each stitch around.

Pull the tail gently to close the center hole completely.

Weave yarn through one or two stitches to secure the tail.

Depending on the pattern, either leave the tail if it's needed for sewing, or weave in ends and either trim the yarn or hide it inside the piece.

Flatten and Work Through Both Thicknesses

Press both layers of the piece's oen end together so that they lie flat on top of each other, aligning the stitches side by side. Work single crochet stitches through 2 opposing stitches together.

Fasten off and leave a long tail for sewing.

Tip: *I use this technique for closing Ears, Arms and Legs – so that they lay flat against the finished piece.*

Sewing Pieces Together

Most crocheters I know do not like sewing. Personally, I prefer crocheting the head and body separately and then sewing them together. In that way, you can add details to each of the pieces before joining them.

NOTES

» The pieces you are sewing together must face the same way, unless instructed otherwise.

» Always use pins to keep the pieces in position. For the symmetrical parts (Arms, Legs & Ears), it's very important to find the best position for both of them on the Body / Head first, before sewing.

» When sewing the Head, Arms or Ears to the Body, I always repeat the sewing process at least 2 times, to make sure that the joins are stable.

» For attaching a flat piece (e.g. Titou Tiger's Muzzle), I sew through both loops of each stitch from the final round of the piece using straight stitches.

» Always keep a long yarn tail from at least one piece when you need to sew pieces together. When sewing both open-ended pieces together (like Body and Head), I prefer keeping long tails from both pieces and repeating the sewing process with both tails.

» When there is no tail to use for sewing, where possible, use the same color yarn of at least one of the pieces.

» Leave a long tail when using a separate strand of yarn for sewing. It is easier to adjust positioning (and pull out if necessary) when the tail is not secured. When the pieces are joined, then secure and weave in the tail ends.

Whipstitch

This stitch is commonly used to join "open" to "open" pieces.

With both pieces right-side facing, insert your needle through a crocheted stitch on the first piece, from front to back.

Step 1: Bring the needle up through the corresponding stitch on the second piece, from back to front.

Step 2: Insert your needle in the next stitch on the first piece from front to back. Repeat Steps 1 & 2.

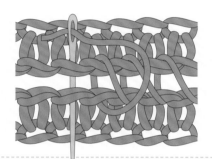

Tip: I use whipstitch to sew the Ears to the Head or to sew the limbs to the Body.

Example: *Sewing the Ear on Head*

» *Pin the Ear in place.*

» *Thread the Ear's yarn tail on needle and insert the needle into the Head, bringing it out on the other side near the Ear's position.*

» *Insert the needle into the edge of the Ear.*

» *Whipstitch evenly across all the Ear's stitches, catching the Head stitches.*

Mattress Stitch

This is a very versatile stitch and can be virtually "invisible" when tugged gently. It can be used for joining most of the types of pieces together.

Both pieces should be right-side facing. Starting on the first piece, insert your needle under a crocheted stitch, from front to back to front.

On the corresponding stitch on the second piece, insert the needle from front to back to front under the stitch.

Step 1: On the first piece, insert your needle in the same place where it came out and bring it up under the next stitch.

Step 2: On the second piece, insert your needle in the same place where it came out and bring it up under the next stitch. Repeat steps 1 & 2.

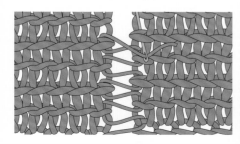

Tip: *When I need to sew open-ended pieces together (or an open-ended piece to a stuffed piece), I use the mattress stitch.*

Example: Sewing the Tail (open-ended) onto Body

» *Position the Tail and pin in place.*

» *Thread the Tail's yarn tail on needle, and tack a few stitches at the pin positions.*

» *Using mattress stitch, evenly sew around, joining Tail to Body.*

Embroidery - Straight Stitch

Straight Stitch

Bring threaded needle up from wrong to right side of fabric at the position you want to start the stitch. Insert the needle back into the fabric at the position you want to end the stitch. Repeat for the remaining stitches.

Note: *For most of the embroidery on my toys, I use the straight stitch.*

To Make a Nose

Make a few horizontal straight stitches, and one straight vertical stitch to the center front of Face or Muzzle to create a nose.

Embroider the Nose using Straight stitches to center front of face or muzzle.

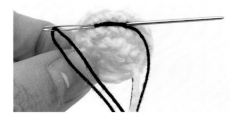

To Make Sleeping Eyes

Using a long strand of embroidery thread and needle, insert the needle in at the neck (leaving a tail for tying), through the head, and bring it out at the first position of the Eye. Insert needle in at the last position of Eye, creating a strand, and bring it out on the round below to start the eyelashes.

Insert needle under the eye strand and then insert into the head on the next round below, to make first eyelash.

Continue making eyelashes.

After the last eyelash, insert the needle through the head, bringing it out at the same place on the neck.

Tie the tails together and hide the tail ends inside the head. A sleeping eye is made. Repeat for other eye.

Projects

Anna
The Little Bunny Girl

Anna likes playing outside in the garden, listening to the sweet songs of the birds and collecting flowers. Mommy made her the cutest bunny outfit ever, and she wears it all the time. Everyone in the family calls her "Little Bunny Girl".

MATERIALS

Scheepjes Softfun

Main Color (MC): Cream (2426)
Color A: Fuchsia (2534)
Color B: Light Pink (2513)
Color C: White (2412)
Brown (2623) - for Hair
Orange (2427) & Yellow Green (2531) - small amounts for Bag

Scheepjes Maxi Sweet Treat (Cotton Thread)

Black Coffee (162) - for embroidery

Sizes C-2 (2.75 mm) (Main Hook) & D-3 (3.25 mm) Crochet Hooks - or sizes suitable for yarn used. (Use Main Hook throughout, unless otherwise stated.)
Yarn Needle
Embroidery Needle
Stitch Markers
Small piece of White Felt
Pink & Black Fabric Pens
White Thread and Needle (for sewing appliqué)
5⁄16" (8 mm) Safety Eyes - 2
Toy Stuffing
Cosmetic Blusher & Brush - for Cheeks

Finished Size
About 7⅞" (20 cm) tall

Skill Level
♥♥♥

HEAD

Round 1: Using MC, make a Magic Ring; ch 1, 8 sc in ring, DO NOT JOIN. (8 sc) Tug tail to tighten ring. Mark last stitch.

Round 2: Inc in each st around. (16 sc) Move marker each round.

Round 3: [Sc in next st, inc in next st] 8 times. (24 sc)

Round 4: [Sc in each of next 2 sts, inc in next st] 8 times. (32 sc)

Round 5: [Sc in each of next 3 sts, inc in next st] 8 times. (40 sc)

Round 6: Sc in each st around. (40 sc)

Round 7: [Sc in each of next 4 sts, inc in next st] 8 times. (48 sc)

Rounds 8-11: *(4 Rounds)* Sc in each st around. (48 sc)

Round 12: [Sc in each of next 7 sts, inc in next st] 6 times. (54 sc)

Rounds 13-15: *(3 Rounds)* Sc in each st around. (54 sc)

Round 16: [Sc in each of next 8 sts, inc in next st] 6 times. (60 sc)

Round 17: [Sc in each of next 8 sts, **sc-dec**] 6 times. (54 sc)

Round 18: Sc in each of next 3 sts, sc-dec, [sc in each of next 7 sts, sc-dec] 5 times, sc in each of next 4 sts. (48 sc)

Round 19: [Sc in each of next 6 sts, sc-dec] 6 times. (42 sc)

Round 20: Sc in each of next 2 sts, sc-dec, [sc in each of next 5 sts, sc-dec] 5 times, sc in each of next 3 sts. (36 sc)

Round 21: [Sc in each of next 4 sts, sc-dec] 6 times. (30 sc)

» Insert Safety Eyes between Rounds 14 & 15, about 9 stitches apart.

» Start stuffing Head, adding more as you go.

Round 22: Sc in next st, sc-dec, [sc in each of next 3 sts, sc-dec] 5 times, sc in each of next 2 sts. (24 sc)

Round 23: [Sc in each of next 2 sts, sc-dec] 6 times. (18 sc) Sl st in next st. Fasten off, leaving a long tail for sewing.

» Using Cotton Thread, embroider an an Eyebrow (2 rounds above Eye), and an Eyelash for each Eye (images 1 & 2).

ARM (Make 2)

Note: *Arms are not stuffed.*

Round 1: Using MC, make a Magic Ring; ch 1, 8 sc in ring, DO NOT JOIN. (8 sc) Tug tail to tighten ring. Mark last stitch, move the marker each round.

Rounds 2-5: *(4 Rounds)* Sc in each st around. (8 sc) At the end of Round 5, change to Color B.

Round 6: Sc in each st around. (8 sc)

Round 7: Working in BLO, [inc in next st, sc in next st] 4 times. (12 sc)

Rounds 8-15: *(8 Rounds)* Sc in each st around. (12 sc)

Round 16: [Sc in next st, sc-dec] 4 times. (8 sc)
Fasten off and close remaining sts, leaving a long tail for sewing.

Arm Detail

Round 1: With hand facing upwards, working in FLO of Round 6, attach Color B to any st (image 3), ch 1, sc in each st around; join with sl st to first sc. (8 sc)

Round 2: Ch 1, inc in same st as joining, sc in next st, [inc in next st, sc in next st] 3 times; fasten off with invisible join (12 sc) (image 4).

LEGS

First Leg

Rounds 1-2: Using Color A, repeat Rounds 1-2 of Head. At the end of Round 2, there are 16 sc.

Round 3: Sc in next st, inc in next st, sc in each of next 4 sts, inc in each of next 4 sts, sc in each of next 4 sts, inc in next st, sc in last st. (22 sc)

Rounds 4-6: *(3 Rounds)* Sc in each st around. (22 sc)

Round 7: Sc in each of next 7 sts, [sc-dec] 4 times, sc in each of next 7 sts. (18 sc)

Round 8: Sc in each of next 5 sts, [sc-dec] 4 times, sc in each of next 5 sts, changing to Color B in last st. (14 sc) Leave the Color A hanging on the outside.

Round 9: Working in BLO, sc in each st around, changing to MC in last st. (14 sc) Leave Color B hanging on the outside (image 5).

Round 10: Working in BLO, [sc each of next 2 sts, sc-dec] 3 times, sc in each of next 2 sts. (11 sc)

» Start stuffing Leg, adding more as you go.

Rounds 11-23: *(13 Rounds)* Sc in each st around. (11 sc)

Round 24: Sc in each of next 10 sts. (10 sc) Leave last st unworked. Fasten off.

Leg Detail

First Round: Working in FLO of Round 9, insert hook in first st and pull up Color B, [ch 2, sl st in next st] 14 times. Fasten off and weave in ends.

Second Round: Working in FLO of Round 8, insert hook in first st and pull up Color A, ch 1, sc in each st around; fasten off with invisible join. (14 sc) (image 6).

Second Leg

Rounds 1-23: Repeat Rounds 1-23 of First Leg

Round 24: Sc in each st around. (11 sc) Do not fasten off MC.

» Repeat Leg Detail on Second Leg.

Round 25: Sc in each of next 5 sts; change to Color B. (5 sc) Leave remaining sts unworked. Fasten off MC. Do not fasten off Color B.

BODY

Round 1: *(Joining Legs)* Working on Second Leg, ch 5 (image 7); working on First Leg, sc in last st made (image 8), sc in each of next 10 sts; working in ch-5, [sc in next ch, inc in next ch] 2 times, sc in last ch; working on Second Leg, sc in each of next 11 sts; working in unused loops on other side of ch-5, [sc in next ch, inc in next ch] 2 times, sc in last ch. (36 sc) Mark last st made. Move marker each round.

Rounds 2-4: *(3 Rounds)* Sc in each st around. (36 sc)

Round 5: [Sc in each of next 4 sts, sc-dec] 6 times. (30 sc)

Rounds 6-10: *(5 Rounds)* Sc in each st around. (30 sc)

» Start stuffing Body, adding more as you go.

Round 11: [Sc in each of next 8 sts, sc-dec] 3 times. (27 sc)

Rounds 12-16: *(5 Rounds)* Sc in each st around. (27 sc)

Round 17: [Sc in each of next 7 sts, sc-dec] 3 times. (24 sc)

Round 18a: *(Collar)* Working in FLO, [ch 4, sl st in next st] 24 times.

Round 18: Working in BLO of Round 17 (image 9), [sc in each of next 2 sts, sc-dec] 6 times. (18 sc) Sl st in next st. Fasten off, leaving a long tail for sewing.

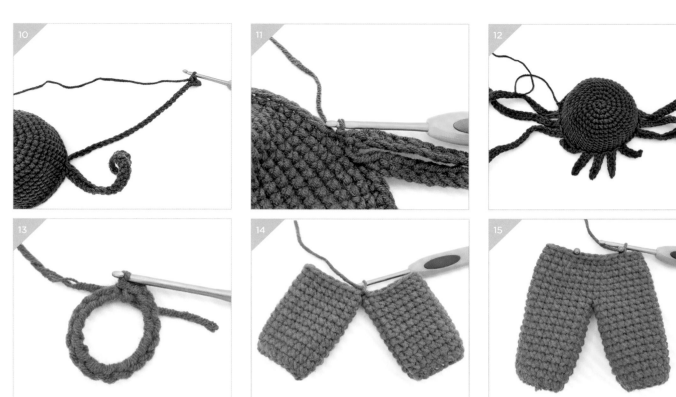

HAIR
(images 10, 11 & 12)

Rounds 1-11: Using Hair Color and larger hook, repeat Rounds 1-11 of Head. At the end of Round 11, there are 48 sc.

Rounds 12-13: *(2 Rounds)* Sc in each st around. (48 sc)

Round 14: *(Hair strands)* [Sl st in next st; ch 20, starting in second ch from hook, sc in each ch across (19 sc); sl st in next st] 3 times, sc in each of next 2 sts, [sl st in next st; ch 6, starting in second ch from hook, sc in each ch across (5 sc); sl st in next st] 5 times , sc in each of next 2 sts, [sl st in next st; ch 20, starting in second ch from hook, sc in each ch across (19 sc); sl st in next st] 3 times, sc in each of next 22 sts. Fasten off, leaving a very long tail for sewing.

OVERALLS

Pants Leg (Make 2)

Round 1: Using Color A and larger hook, ch 18; join with a sl st to first ch to make a ring (image 13); ch 1, sc in each ch around; join with sl st to first sc. (18 sc) Join all rounds in this manner.

Rounds 2-12: *(11 Rounds)* Ch 1, sc in each st around; join. (18 sc) At the end of Round 12, for the first Pants Leg, fasten off. For the second Pants Leg, do not fasten off.

Pants

Round 1: *(Joining Legs)* Working on the first Leg, sl st in last st made (image 14), ch 1, sc in each st around; working on the second Leg, sc in each st around; join. (36 sc)

Rounds 2-5: *(4 Rounds)* Ch 1, sc in each st around; join. (36 sc)

Round 6: Ch 1, [sc in each of next 4 sts, sc-dec] 6 times; join. (30 sc)

Round 7: Ch 1, sc in each st around; join. (30 sc) Fasten off, leaving a long tail for sewing.

Bib

Mark the center 8 sts at front of Pants (image 15).

Rows 1: Attach Color A to first marked st, ch 1, sc in same st, sc in each of next 7 sts. (8 sc)

Rows 2-4: *(3 Rows)* Ch 1, turn, sc in each st across. (8 sc) At the end of Row 4, do not fasten off.

Straps: Ch 20 (image 16), starting in the second ch from hook, sl st in each ch across *(first Strap);* working in last row of Bib (image 17), sc in each of next 6 sts; ch 20 (image 18), starting in the second ch from hook, sl st in each ch across *(second Strap)*, sl st in last st of Bib. Fasten off and weave in ends (image 19).

Bunny Appliqué

Using a small piece of white felt, trim to shape of a bunny's head. Using fabric pens, draw the ears, eyes & whiskers. Sew it to front leg on Overalls (image 20).

ASSEMBLY (use photos as guide)

Arms - Position the Arms on either side of the Body, one round below Collar. Using long tails and yarn needle, sew them in place (image 21).

Head - Sew Head to Body.

Hair - Place Hair on Head, using pins to keep it in place (image 22). Braid the long strands on either side of head (image 23). Using long tail and needle, sew the strands in place (image 24).

Overalls - Place Overalls on Body, and cross the Straps at the back. Using the tail from the Pants, sew the Straps in place (image 25).

Face - Using a small makeup brush, apply blusher to the cheeks.

ACCESSORIES

Carrot Bag

Round 1: Using Orange and larger hook, make a Magic Ring; ch 1, 6 sc in ring, DO NOT JOIN. (6 sc) Tug tail to tighten ring. Mark last stitch.
Round 2: [Inc in next st, sc in each of next 2 sts] 2 times.

(8 sc) Move marker each round.

Round 3: [Sc in each of next 3 sts, inc in next st] 2 times. (10 sc)

Round 4: [Sc in each of next 4 sts, inc in next st] 2 times. (12 sc)

Round 5: [Sc in each of next 4 sts, sc-dec] 2 times. (10 sc)

Round 6: [Sc in each of next 3 sts, sc-dec] 2 times, hanging to Green in last st. (8 sc)

Round 7: Working in FLO, [ch 2, sl st in next st] 8 times, ch 45 *(strap)*. Fasten off, leaving a long tail for sewing.

» Using tail and needle, sew strap to Bag (image 26).

» Using Cotton Thread, embroider a few small lines on Bag, using straight stitches (image 27).

BUNNY HAT

Round 1: Using Color C and larger hook, make a Magic Ring; ch 2, 12 hdc in ring; tug tail to tighten ring; join with sl st to first hdc. (12 hdc) Join all rounds in this manner.

Round 2: Ch 2, 2 hdc in each st around; join. (24 hdc)

Round 3: Ch 2, [hdc in next st, 2 hdc in next st] 12 times; join. (36 hdc)

Round 4: Ch 2, [hdc in each of next 2 sts, 2 hdc in next st] 12 times; join. (48 hdc)

Round 5: Ch 2, [hdc in each of next 11 sts, 2 hdc in next st] 4 times; join. (52 hdc)

Rounds 6-10: *(5 Rounds)* Ch 2, hdc in each st around; join. (52 hdc)

Round 11: Ch 2, [hdc in each of next 3 sts, 2 hdc in next st] 13 times; join. (65 hdc) Fasten off and weave in ends.

Inner Ear (Make 2)

Using Color B and larger hook, ch 9, starting in the second ch from hook, sc in each of next 3 ch, hdc in each of next 3 ch, dc in next ch, 5 dc in the last ch; working in unused loops on other side of starting ch, dc in next ch, hdc in each of next 3 ch, sc in each of next 3 ch. (19 sts) Fasten off.

Outer Ear (Make 2)

Using Color C and larger hook, repeat Inner Ear, but do not fasten off (image 28).

» Holding Inner and Outer Ear with wrong sides together and Inner Ear facing, working through both thicknesses, matching sts and shaping, sc in each st across. (19 sc) Fasten off, leaving a long tail for sewing (images 29 & 30).

» Sew the Ears to Round 5 of Hat, 9 sts apart (image 31).

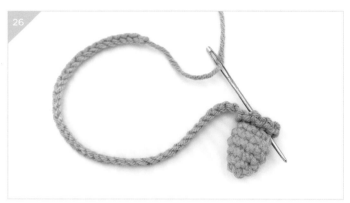

Billy The Cat

Billy, the Cat, spends his weekends at the lake. He loves fishing! Today was his lucky day and he came home with a basket full of fish. He's going to have a very good dinner!

MATERIALS

Scheepjes Softfun

Main Color (MC): White (2412)
Color A: Cream (2426)
Color B: Olive Green (2616)
Color C: Mustard (2621)

(for Little Fishes)
Small amounts of
Yellow (2518), Orange (2427),
Green (2531), Baby Blue (2613),
Light Peach (2466) & Navy Blue (2489)

Scheepjes Stone Washed

Yellow Jasper (809) - for Basket

Scheepjes Merino Soft

Gauguin (619) - for Bow Tie

Scheepjes Maxi Sweet Treat (Cotton Thread)

Black Coffee (162) - for embroidery

Size C-2 (2.75 mm) Crochet Hook - or size
suitable for yarn used.
Yarn Needle
Embroidery Needle
Stitch Markers
⁵⁄₁₆" (8 mm) Safety Eyes - 2
Toy Stuffing
Cosmetic Blusher & Brush - for Cheeks
10 cm piece of Wire - for Fishing Rod

Finished Size
About 5½" (14 cm) tall

Skill Level

LEG (Make 2)

Round 1: Using Color A, make a Magic Ring; ch 1, 8 sc in ring, DO NOT JOIN. (8 sc) Tug tail to tighten ring. Mark last stitch.

Round 2: Inc in each st around, changing to MC in last st. Fasten off Color A. (16 sc) Move marker each round.

Round 3: Sc in next st, inc in next st, sc in each of next 5 sts, inc in each of next 2 sts, sc in each of next 5 sts, inc in next st, sc in next st. (20 sc)

Round 4: Sc in each st around. (20 sc)

Round 5: Sc in each of next 6 sts, [**sc-dec**] 4 times, sc in each of next 6 sts. (16 sc)

Round 6: [Sc in each of next 4 sts, sc-dec] 2 times, sc in each of next 4 sts. (14 sc)

Round 7: Sc in each of next 6 sts, sc-dec, sc in each of next 6 sts. (13 sc)

Round 8: Sc in each of next 6 sts, inc in next st, sc in each of next 6 sts. (14 sc)

  » Stuff Leg.

Last Row Flatten the last round and working through both thicknesses, sc in each of next 7 sc.
Fasten off, leaving a long tail for sewing.

  » Using Cotton Thread and needle, embroider 3 straight lines (for toes) at Round 3 of each Leg (image 1).

ARM (Make 2)

Round 1: Using MC, make a Magic Ring; ch 1, 6 sc in ring, DO NOT JOIN. (6 sc) Tug tail to tighten ring. Mark last stitch.

Round 2: [Inc in next st, sc in each of next 2 sts] 2 times. (8 sc) Move marker each round.

Round 3: Sc in each st around. (8 sc)

Round 4: [Sc in next st, inc in next st] 4 times. (12 sc)

Rounds 5-6: (2 Rounds) Sc in each st around. (12 sc)
At the end of Round 6, change to Color B. Fasten off MC.

Round 7 Sc in each st around, changing to Color A in last st. Do not fasten off Color B. (12 sc)

Round 8: [Sc in each of next 2 sts, inc in next st] 4 times, changing to Color B in last st. (16 sc)

Round 9: Sc in each st around, changing to Color A in last st.

Fasten off Color B. (16 sc)

  » Stuff Arm lightly.

Round 10: [Sc-dec] 8 times. (8 sc) Fasten off and close remaining sts, leaving a long tail for sewing.
(image 2 - Arms & Ears)

EAR (Make 2)

Note: *The colored font indicates where Color A is used. Use the Stranding Method for the color changes.*

Round 1: Using Color C, make a Magic Ring; ch 1, 6 sc in ring, DO NOT JOIN. (6 sc) Tug tail to tighten ring. Mark last stitch.

Round 2: [Inc in next st, sc in next st] 3 times. (9 sc) Move marker each round.

Round 3: Inc in next st, sc in each of next 2 sts, inc in next st; change to Color A, sc in next st; change to Color C, sc in next st, inc in next st, sc in each of next 2 sts. (12 sc)

Round 4: Sc in each of next 5 sts; change to Color A, sc in each of next 3 sts; change to Color C, sc in each of next 4 sts. (12 sc)

Round 5: Sc in each of next 3 sts, inc in next st, sc in next st; change to Color A, sc in each of next 2 sts, inc in next st; change to Color C, sc in each of next 3 sts, inc in next st. (15 sc)

Round 6: Sc in each of next 4 sts, inc in next st, sc in next st; change to Color A, sc in each of next 3 sts, inc in next st; change to Color C, sc in each of next 4 sts, inc in next st. (18 sc) Sl st in next st. Fasten off, leaving a long tail for sewing.

TAIL

Rounds 1-2: Using Color C, repeat Rounds 1-2 of Ears. At the end of Round 2, there are 9 sc.

Rounds 3-5: *(3 Rounds)* Sc in each st around. (9 sc) At the end of Round 5, change to MC.

  » Stuff Tail up to Round 5. Do not stuff the rest of Tail.

Rounds 6-26: *(21 Rounds)* Sc in each st around. (9 sc)

Last Row: Flatten the last round and working through both thicknesses, sc in each of next 4 sc. Fasten off, leaving a long tail for sewing.

HEAD & BODY

Note: *The colored font indicates where Color C is used. Use the Cut & Tie Method for the color changes.*

Round 1: Starting at Head, using MC, make a Magic Ring; ch 1, 8 sc in ring, DO NOT JOIN. (8 sc) Tug tail to tighten ring. Mark last stitch.

Round 2: [Inc in next st] 4 times; change to Color C, [inc in next st] 4 times, change to MC. (16 sc) Move marker each round.

Round 3: [Sc in next st, inc in next st] 4 times; change to Color C, [sc in next st, inc in next st] 4 times, change to MC. (24 sc)

Round 4: [Sc in each of next 2 sts, inc in next st] 4 times; change to Color C, [sc in each of next 2 sts, inc in next st] 4 times, change to MC. (32 sc)

Round 5: [Sc in each of next 3 sts, inc in next st] 4 times; change to Color C, [sc in each of next 3 sts, inc in next st] 4 times, change to MC. (40 sc)

Round 6: [Sc in each of next 4 sts, inc in next st] 4 times; change to Color C, [sc in each of next 4 sts, inc in next st] 4 times, change to MC. (48 sc)

Rounds 7-9: *(3 Rounds)* Sc in each of next 24 sts; change to Color C, sc in each of next 24 sts, change to MC. (48 sc)

Round 10: Sc in each of next 25 sts; change to Color C, sc in each of next 22 sts, change to MC, sc in next st. (48 sc)

Round 11: [Sc in each of next 7 sts, inc in next st] 3 times, sc in each of next 2 sts; change to Color C, sc in each of next 5 sts, inc in next st, sc in each of next 7 sts, inc in next st, sc in each of next 6 sts; change to MC, sc in next st, inc in next st. (54 sc)

Round 12: Sc in each of next 30 sts; change to Color C, sc in each of next 20 sts, change to MC, sc in each of next 4 sts. (54 sc)

Round 13: Sc in each of next 31 sts; change to Color C, sc in each of next 18 sts, change to MC, sc in each of next 5 sts. (54 sc) Fasten off Color C.

Round 14: Sc in each st around. (54 sc)

Round 15: [Sc in each of next 8 sts, inc in next st] 6 times. (60 sc)

Rounds 16-17: *(2 Rounds)* Sc in each st around. (60 sc)

Round 18: [Sc in each of next 8 sts, sc-dec] 6 times. (54 sc)

Round 19: Sc in each of next 3 sts, sc-dec, [sc in each of next 7 sts, sc-dec] 5 times, sc in each of next 4 sts. (48 sc)

Round 20: [Sc in each of next 6 sts, sc-dec] 6 times. (42 sc)

Round 21: Sc in each of next 2 sts, sc-dec, [sc in each of next 5 sts, sc-dec] 5 times, sc in each of next 3 sts. (36 sc)

Round 22: [Sc in each of next 4 sts, sc-dec] 6 times. (30 sc)

Round 23: [Sc in each of next 3 sts, sc-dec] 6 times, change to Color B. Fasten off MC. (24 sc)

» Insert Safety Eyes between Rounds 15 & 16, about 10 stitches apart.

» Stuff Head firmly, adding more to Body as you go.

Round 24: With Color B, [sc in each of next 2 sts, inc in next st] 8 times, change to Color A. (32 sc) *Alternate Color A and Color B every round.*

Rounds 25-26: *(2 Rounds)* Sc in each st around. (32 sc)

Round 27: [Sc in each of next 3 sts, inc in next st] 8 times. (40 sc)

Rounds 28-29 *(2 Rounds)* Sc in each st around. (40 sc)

Round 30: [Sc in each of next 4 sts, inc in next st] 8 times. (48 sc)

Rounds 31-32: *(2 Rounds)* Sc in each st around. (48 sc)

Round 33: [Sc in each of next 11 sts, inc in next st] 4 times. (52 sc)

Round 34: Sc in each st around, changing to MC in last st. (52 sc) Fasten off Color A. Leave Color B hanging on the outside (image 3).

Round 35: With MC, working in BLO, [sc in each of next 12 sts, inc in next st] around. (56 sc)

Round 36: Sc in each of next 6 sts; change to Color C, sc in each of next 18 sts; change to MC, sc in each of next 32 sts. (56 sc)

Round 37: Sc in each of next 5 sts; change to Color C, sc in each of next 20 sts; change to MC, sc in each of next 31 sts. (56 sc)

Round 38: Sc in each of next 4 sts; change to Color C, sc in next st, [sc-dec, sc in each of next 5 sts] 3 times; change to MC, [sc-dec, sc in each of next 5 sts] 4 times, sc-dec. (48 sc)

Round 39: Sc in each of next 4 sts; change to Color C, sc in each of next 19 sts; change to MC, sc in each of next 25 sts. (48 sc)

Round 40: Sc in each of next 4 sts; change to Color C, [sc-dec, sc in each of next 4 sts] 3 times; change to MC, [sc-dec, sc in each of next 4 sts] 4 times, sc-dec. (40 sc)

Round 41: [Sc in each of next 3 sts, sc-dec] 8 times. (32 sc)

Round 42: [Sc in each of next 2 sts, sc-dec] 8 times. (24 sc)

Round 43: [Sc in next st, sc-dec] 8 times. (16 sc)

Round 44: [Sc-dec] 8 times. (8 sc)

» Finish stuffing Body.

Fasten off and close remaining sts, weaving in end.

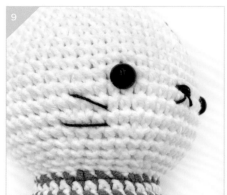

Sweater Edging: Picking up Color B, working in FLO of Round 34 (image 4), sl st in each st around (image 5). Fasten off and weave in ends (image 6).

BOW TIE

Row 1: (Right/Wrong Side) Using Gauguin, ch 7, starting in the third ch from the hook *(skipped chs count as first dc)*, dc in each ch across. (5 dc)

Rows 2-4: *(3 Rows)* Ch 3, turn, dc in each st across. (5 dc) Fasten off and weave in ends.

» Wrap a small length of Yellow yarn tightly around the center of the Bow Tie (between Rows 2 & 3). Secure and leave a long tail for sewing (image 7).

ASSEMBLY (use photos as guide)

Face - Using Cotton Thread, embroider a Nose between the Eyes (image 8). Embroider Whiskers below each eye, using Straight Stitches (images 9 & 10).

Using a small makeup brush, apply blusher to the cheeks.

Ears - Position Ears on either side of Head (between Rounds 4 & 10) and sew in place (image 11).

Arms - Position Arms on either side of Body, two rounds below Neck. Using long tails and yarn needle, sew them in place (image 12).

Legs - Position and sew Legs on either side of Body

(images 13 & 14).

Tail - Position and sew Tail to center back at base of Body. Tack a few rounds of the Tail to the Body (images 15 & 16).

Bow Tie - Sew Bow Tie below Neck.

ACCESSORIES

Basket

Round 1: Using Yellow Jasper, make a Magic Ring; ch 1, 8 sc in ring; join with sl st to first sc. (8 sc) Join all rounds in this manner. Tug tail to tighten ring.

Round 2: Ch 1, inc in each st around; join. (16 sc)

Round 3: Ch 1, [sc in next st, inc in next st] 8 times; join. (24 sc)

Round 4: Ch 1, [sc in each of next 2 sts, inc in next st] 8 times; join. (32 sc)

Round 5: Working in BLO, ch 1, sc in each st around; join. (32 sc)

Rounds 6-8: *(3 Rounds)* Ch 1, sc in each st around; join. (32 sc)

Round 9: Ch 2, [hdc in next st, ch 1, skip next st] 16 times; join. Fasten off and weave in ends.

(image 17 - Basket, Fishes & Fishing Rod)

Fish (Make 6 - one in each color)

Round 1: Using Color A, make a Magic Ring; ch 1, 6 sc in ring, DO NOT JOIN. (6 sc) Tug tail to tighten ring. Mark last stitch.

Round 2: [Inc in next st, sc in each of next 2 sts] 2 times. (8 sc) Move marker each round.

Round 3: Sc in each st around, changing to Fish color in last st. (8 sc)

Round 4: Sc in each of next 3 sts, inc in next st, sc in each of next 4 sts. (9 sc)

Rounds 5-6: *(2 Rounds)* Sc in each st around. (9 sc)

Round 7: Sc in each of next 3 sts, sc-dec, sc in each of next 4 sts. (8 sc)

» Stuff Fish lightly.

Round 8: [Sc in each of next 2 sts, sc-dec] 2 times, changing to Color A in last st. (6 sc)

Round 9: Inc in each st around. (12 sc)
Fasten off, leaving a long tail.

» Flatten last round. Using long tail and yarn needle, matching stitches sew across last round to close (image 18). Weave in ends.

» Using Cotton Thread and needle, embroider Eyes on each fish.

Fishing Rod

Bend the tip of the wire to form a loop. Using a length of Cotton Thread, attach one end to the wire loop and the other end to a fish.

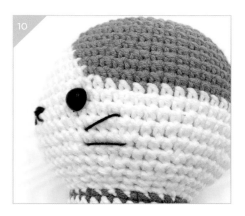

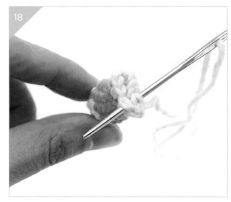

Bobbi Puppy

Bobbi Puppy is the kindest lad in town. On sunny afternoons, you'll find him sitting on the river bank, telling stories of his wonderful adventures to all the children. He has many other talents too, including playing the piano and painting beautiful sunsets.

MATERIALS

Scheepjes Stone Washed

Main Color (MC): Yellow Jasper (809)
Color A: Moon Stone (801)

Scheepjes Softfun

Color B: Yellow Green (2531)

Scheepjes Softfun Denim

Color C: Brown (510)

Scheepjes Merino Soft

Gauguin (619) - for Hat & Bow Tie

Size C-2 (2.75 mm) Crochet Hook - or size suitable for yarn used.
Yarn Needle
Stitch Markers
⅜" (10 mm) Safety Eyes - 2
Small Buttons - 2
Thread and needle - for sewing on buttons
Toy Stuffing
Cosmetic Blusher & Brush - for Cheeks

Finished Size
About 7⅞" (20 cm) tall

Skill Level
♥

BODY

Round 1: Using MC, make a Magic Ring; ch 1, 6 sc in ring, DO NOT JOIN. (6 sc) Tug tail to tighten ring. Mark last stitch.

Round 2: Inc in each st around. (12 sc)
Move marker each round.

Round 3: [Sc in next st, inc in next st] 6 times. (18 sc)

Round 4: [Sc in each of next 2 sts, inc in next st] 6 times. (24 sc)

Round 5: [Sc in each of next 3 sts, inc in next st] 6 times. (30 sc)

Round 6: [Sc in each of next 4 sts, inc in next st] 6 times. (36 sc)

Round 7: Sc in each of next 2 sts, inc in next st, [sc in each of next 5 sts, inc in next st] 5 times, sc in each of next 3 sts. (42 sc)

Round 8: [Sc in each of next 6 sts, inc in next st] 6 times. (48 sc)

Round 9: Working in BLO, sc in each st around. (48 sc)

Round 10: [Sc in each of next 7 sts, inc in next st] 6 times. (54 sc)

Rounds 11-15: (5 Rounds) Sc in each st around. (54 sc) At the end of Round 15, change to Color B.

Round 16: Sc in each st around. (54 sc)

Round 17: Working in BLO, sc in each st around. (54 sc)

Round 18: Sc in each st around. (54 sc)

Round 19: [Sc in each of next 7 sts, **sc-dec**] 6 times. (48 sc)

Rounds 20-27: (8 Rounds) Sc in each st around. (48 sc)

Round 28: [Sc in each of next 6 sts, sc-dec] 6 times. (42 sc)

» Start stuffing Body, adding more as you go.

Rounds 29-31: (3 Rounds) Sc in each st around. (42 sc)

Round 32: [Sc in each of next 5 sts, sc-dec] 6 times. (36 sc)

Round 33: Sc in each st around. (36 sc)

Round 34: [Sc in each of next 4 sts, sc-dec] 6 times. (30 sc)

Round 35: Sc in each st around. (30 sc)

Round 36: [Sc in each of next 3 sts, sc-dec] 6 times. (24 sc)

Round 37: Hdc in each of next 3 sts, dc in each of next 3 sts, hdc in each of next 3 sts, sc in each of next 15 sts. (24 sts)

Round 38: Sc in each of next 9 sts. (9 sc) Leave remaining sts unworked. Sl st in next st. Fasten off, leaving a long tail for sewing.

Note: *The hdc/dc/hdc-sts on Round 37 will be at the back of the Body and the sc stitches at the front.*

Shirt Detail

Working in the FLO of Round 16, attach Color B to the first st (image 1), sl st in each st around. Fasten off and weave in ends (image 2).

ARM (Make 2)

Rounds 1-2: Using Color A, repeat Rounds 1-2 of Body. At the end of Round 2, there are 12 sc.

Round 3: [Sc in each of next 3 sts, inc in next st] 3 times, changing to MC in last st. (15 sc)

Rounds 4-12: (9 Rounds) Sc in each st around. (15 sc) At the end of Round 12, change to Color B.

Round 13: Sc in each st around. (15 sc)

» Start stuffing the Arm, adding more as you go.

Round 14: Working in BLO, sc in each st around. (15 sc)

Rounds 15-28: *(14 Rounds)* Sc in each st around. (15 sc)
Round 29: [Sc in each of next 3 sts, sc-dec] 3 times. (12 sc)
Rounds 30-31: *(2 Rounds)* Sc in each st around. (12 sc)
Round 32: [Sc-dec] 6 times. (6 sc)

» Finish stuffing Arm.

Fasten off and close remaining sts, leaving a long tail for sewing.

Arm Detail

Working in the FLO of Round 13, attach Color B to first st (image 3), sl st in each st around. Fasten off and weave in ends.

(image 4 - Arms & Legs)

LEG (Make 2)

Rounds 1-4: Using Color A, repeat Rounds 1-4 of Body. At the end of Round 4, there are 24 sc. Change to MC.
Round 5: Sc in each st around. (24 sc)
Round 6: Sc in each of next 6 st, [sc in next st, sc-dec] 4 times, sc in each of next 6 st. (20 sc)
Rounds 7-15: *(9 Rounds)* Sc in each st around. (20 sc)
Round 16: [Sc in each of next 8 sts, sc-dec] 2 times. (18 sc)

» Start stuffing Leg, adding more as you go.

Rounds 17-24: *(8 Rounds)* Sc in each st around. (18 sc)
Round 25: [Sc in each of next 7 sts, sc-dec] 2 times. (16 sc)
Rounds 26-33: *(8 Rounds)* Sc in each st around. (16 sc)
Round 34: [Sc in each of next 2 sts, sc-dec] 4 times. (12 sc)
Round 35: [Sc in next st, sc-dec] 4 times. (8 sc)

» Finish stuffing Leg.

Fasten off and close remaining sts, leaving a long tail for sewing.

HEAD

Rounds 1-5: Using Color A, repeat Rounds 1-5 of Body. At the end of Round 5, there are 30 sc.
Round 6: Sc in each st around. (30 sc)
Round 7: [Sc in each of next 4 sts, inc in next st] 6 times. (36 sc)
Round 8: Sc in each st around. (36 sc)
Round 9: [Sc in each of next 5 sts, inc in next st] 6 times, changing to MC in last st. (42 sc)
Round 10: Sc in each of next 16 sts, [inc in next st, sc in next st] 6 times, sc in each of next 14 sts. (48 sc)
Round 11: Sc in each st around. (48 sc)
Round 12: Sc in each of next 18 sts, [inc in next st, sc in each of next 2 sts] 5 times, sc in each of next 15 sts. (53 sc)
Round 13: Sc in each st around. (53 sc)
Round 14: Sc in each of next 17 sts, [inc in next st, sc in each of next 3 sts] 6 times, sc in each of next 12 sts. (59 sc)

Rounds 15-24: *(10 Rounds)* Sc in each st around. (59 sc)
Round 25: Sc in each of next 4 sts, [sc in each of next 8 sts, sc-dec] 5 times, sc in each of next 5 sts. (54 sc)
Round 26: Sc in each st around. (54 sc)
Round 27: [Sc in each of next 7 sts, sc-dec] 6 times. (48 sc)

» Insert Safety Eyes between Rounds 11 & 12, the first Eye is between 16th & 17th stitch, the second Eye between 33rd & 34th stitch.

Round 28: Sc in each st around. (48 sc)

» Start stuffing Head, adding more as you go.

Round 29: [Sc in each of next 6 sts, sc-dec] 6 times. (42 sc)
Round 30: Sc in each st around. (42 sc)
Round 31: [Sc in each of next 5 sts, sc-dec] 6 times. (36 sc)
Round 32: Sc in each of next 2 sts, sc-dec, [sc in each of next 4 sts, sc-dec] 5 times, sc in each of next 2 sts. (30 sc)
Round 33: [Sc in each of next 3 sts, sc-dec] 6 times. (24 sc)
Round 34: [Sc in each of next 2 sts, sc-dec] 6 times. (18 sc)
Round 35: [Sc in each of next st, sc-dec] 6 times. (12 sc)
Round 36: [Sc-dec] 6 times. (6 sc)

» Finish stuffing Head.

Fasten off and close remaining sts. Mark the center of face between the Eyes with a pin (image 5).

EAR (Make 2)

Rounds 1-5: Using Color C, repeat Rounds 1-5 of Body. At the end of Round 5, there are 30 sc.
Rounds 6-8: *(3 Rounds)* Sc in each st around. (30 sc)
Round 9: [Sc in each of next 3 sts, sc-dec] 6 times. (24 sc)
Rounds 10-11: *(2 Rounds)* Sc in each st around. (24 sc)
Round 12: [Sc in each of next 2 sts, sc-dec] 6 times. (18 sc)
Rounds 13-15: *(3 Rounds)* Sc in each st around. (18 sc)
Round 16: [Sc in next st, sc-dec] 6 times. (12 sc)

Last Row: Flatten the last round and working through both thicknesses, sc in each of next 6 sc. Fasten off, leaving a long tail for sewing.

TAIL

Rounds 1-2: Using Color C, repeat Rounds 1-2 of Body. At the end of Round 2, there are 12 sc.
Round 3: [Sc in each of next 3 sts, inc in next st] 3 times. (15 sc)
Rounds 4-6: *(3 Rounds)* Sc in each st around. (15 sc)
Round 7: [Sc in each of next 3 sts, sc-dec] 3 times. (12 sc)
Rounds 8-10: *(3 Rounds)* Sc in each st around. (12 sc)
Round 11: [Sc in next st, sc-dec] 4 times. (8 sc)
Rounds 12-13: *(2 Rounds)* Sc in each st around. (8 sc)
Last Row: Flatten the last round and working through both thicknesses, sc in each of next 4 sc. Fasten off, leaving a long tail for sewing.

NOSE

Rounds 1-2: Using Color C, repeat Rounds 1-2 of Body. At the end of Round 2, there are 12 sc.
Round 3: Sc in each st around. Sl st in next st. Fasten off, leaving a long tail for sewing.

BOW TIE

Row 1: *(Right Side)* Using Gauguin, ch 7, starting in the third ch from the hook, dc in each ch across. (5 dc)
Rows 2-5: (4 Rows) Ch 3, turn, dc in each st across. (5 dc) At the end of Row 5, fasten off and weave in ends (image 6).

» Wrap a small length of MC tightly around the center of the Bow Tie (around Row 3). Secure and leave a long tail for sewing.

(image 7 - Bow Tie & Hat)

HAT

Round 1: Using Gauguin, make a Magic Ring; ch 1, 8 sc in ring, DO NOT JOIN. (8 sc) Tug tail to tighten ring. Mark last stitch.

Round 2: Inc in each st around. (16 sc) Move marker each round.
Round 3: [Sc in next st, inc in next st] 8 times. (24 sc)
Round 4: [Sc in each of next 2 sts, inc in next st] 8 times. (32 sc)
Round 5: Working in BLO, sc in each st around. (32 sc)
Round 6-8: *(3 Rounds)* Sc in each st around. (32 sc)
Round 9: Working in FLO, ch 2 (does not count as first st), dc in first st, 2 dc in next st, [dc in next st, 2 dc in next st] 15 times; join with sl st to first dc. (48 dc) Fasten off and weave in ends.

Note: *If you would like to secure the Hat on Head, fasten off leaving a long tail. Use the long tail to sew the Hat onto Head*

ASSEMBLY (use photos as guide)

Nose - Position the Nose on Head at Rounds 1 & 4. Using long tail, sew in place (stuffing lightly before closing), and embroider a straight stitch below Nose (image 8).

Ears - Position Ears on either side of Head at Rounds 22 & 27, about 17 sts apart, and sew in place (images 9 & 10).

Eyebrows - Using a double strand of Color C, embroider a straight stitch, one round above each Eye (images 11 & 12).

Body - Position and sew the Body to Rounds 18 & 25 of the Head, positioning the back of the body towards the back of the head, stuffing firmly before closing.

Arms - Position the Arms on either side of the Body (one round below Neck). Using long tails and yarn needle, sew them in place.

Legs - Pin the Legs on either side of the Body in a sitting position at Rounds 9 & 13. Using long tails and yarn needle, sew them in place (image 13).

Tail - Sew Tail at center back of Body, to the front loops of Round 8 (image 14).

Bow Tie & Buttons - Sew the Bow Tie below Neck, and sew the Buttons to front of Body (image 15).

Face - Using a small makeup brush, apply blusher to the cheeks.

Cocola The Koala

Deep in the forest, the Koala family is having a big party today in honor of Cocola. This young lad is heading out to sea on a big boat - to become a true sailor man. We wish him all the luck in the world and "bon voyage"!

MATERIALS

Scheepjes Softfun

Main Color (MC): Light Grey (2530)
Color A: Black Grey (2532)
Color B: Cream (2426)
Color C: Navy Blue (2489)
Color D: White (2412)
Red (2410) - small amount for Hat & Neck Tie

Size C-2 (2.75 mm) Crochet Hook - or size suitable for yarn used.
Yarn Needle
Stitch Markers
½" (12 mm) Safety Eyes - 2
Small Button - 1 - for Hat
Thread and needle - for sewing on button
Toy Stuffing
Cosmetic Blusher & Brush - for Cheeks

Finished Size
About 7⅞" (20 cm) tall

Skill Level
♥

HEAD

Round 1: Using MC, make a Magic Ring; ch 1, 8 sc in ring, DO NOT JOIN. (8 sc) Tug tail to tighten ring. Mark last st.

Round 2: Inc in each st around. (16 sc) Move marker each round.

Round 3: [Sc in next st, inc in next st] 8 times. (24 sc)

Round 4: [Sc in each of next 2 sts, inc in next st] 8 times. (32 sc)

Round 5: [Sc in each of next 3 sts, inc in next st] 8 times. (40 sc)

Round 6: [Sc in each of next 4 sts, inc in next st] 8 times. (48 sc)

Rounds 7-9: *(3 Rounds)* Sc in each st around. (48 sc)

Round 10: [Sc in each of next 5 sts, inc in next st] 8 times. (56 sc)

Rounds 11-17: *(7 Rounds)* Sc in each st around. (56 sc)

Round 18: [Sc in each of next 6 sts, inc in next st] 8 times. (64 sc)

Round 19-22: *(4 Rounds)* Sc in each st around. (64 sc)

Round 23: [Sc in each of next 6 sts, **sc-dec**] 8 times. (56 sc)

Round 24: [Sc in each of next 5 sts, sc-dec] 8 times. (48 sc)

Round 25: [Sc in each of next 6 sts, sc-dec] 6 times. (42 sc)

Round 26: [Sc in each of next 5 sts, sc-dec] 6 times. (36 sc)

Round 27: [Sc in each of next 4 sts, sc-dec] 6 times.(30 sc) Sl st in next st. Fasten off, leaving a long tail for sewing.

» Insert Safety Eyes between Rounds 16 & 17, about 11 stitches apart.

» Stuff Head firmly.

NOSE

Round 1: Using Color A, ch 5, starting in the second ch from hook, sc in each of next 3 ch, 3 sc in the last ch; working in unused loops on other side of starting ch, sc in each of next 2 ch, 2 sc in the last ch. (10 sc). Mark last st and move marker each round.

Rounds 2-4: *(3 Rounds)* Sc in each st around. (10 sc).

Round 5: [Sc in each of next 3 sts, sc-dec] 2 times. (8 sc) Fasten off and close remaining sts, leaving a long tail for sewing.

EAR (Make 2)

Note: *Use the Stranding Method for the color changes.*

Round 1: Using Color B, make a Magic Ring; ch 1, 8 sc in ring, DO NOT JOIN. (8 sc) Tug tail to tighten ring.

Round 2: [2 sc in next st] 4 times; change to MC, [2 sc in next st] 4 times, change to Color B. (16 sc)

Round 3: [Sc in next st, inc in next st] 4 times; change to MC, [sc in next st, inc in next st] 4 times, change to Color B. (24 sc)

Round 4: [Sc in each of next 2 sts, inc in next st] 4 times; change to MC, [sc in each of next 2 sts, inc in next st] 4 times, change to Color B. (32 sc)

Round 5: [Sc in each of next 3 sts, inc in next st] 4 times; change to MC, [sc in each of next 3 sts, inc in next st] 4 times, change to Color B. (40 sc)

Round 6: Sc in each of next 2 sts, inc in next st, [sc in each of next 4 sts, inc in next st] 3 times, sc in each of next 2 sts; change to MC, sc in each of next 2 sts, inc in next st, [sc in each of next 4 sts, inc in next st] 3 times, sc in each of next 2 sts, change to Color B. (48 sc)

Round 7: [Sc in each of next 5 sts, inc in next st] 4 times, change to MC, [sc in each of next 5 sts, inc in next st] 4 times. (56 sc) Fasten off Color B.

Last Row: Fold the Ears in half and working through both thicknesses, sc in each of next 28 sc. Fasten off, leaving a long tail for sewing (images 1 & 2).

ARM (Make 2)

Round 1: Using MC, make a Magic Ring; ch 1, 8 sc in ring, DO NOT JOIN. (8 sc) Tug tail to tighten ring. Mark last stitch.

Round 2: [Sc in next st, inc in next st] 4 times. (12 sc) Move marker each round.

Round 3: [Sc in each of next 5 sts, inc in next st] 2 times. (14 sc)

Rounds 4-9: *(6 Rounds)* Sc in each st around. (14 sc) At the end of Round 9, change to Color C.

Round 10: Sc in each st around. (14 sc)

Round 11: Working in BLO, sc in each st around, change to Color D. (14 sc)

Alternate Color D and Color C every two rounds.

Rounds 12-17: *(6 Rounds)* Sc in each st around. (14 sc) Fasten off Color C.

» Stuff Arm lightly.

Last Row: Flatten the last round and working through both thicknesses, with Color D, sc in each of next 7 sc. Fasten off, leaving a long tail for sewing.

Arm Detail

With hand facing upwards, working in FLO of Round 10, attach Color C to any st (image 3), ch 1, sc in each st around; fasten off with invisible join. (14 sc) (image 4).

LEGS

First Leg

Rounds 1-4: Using Color A, repeat Rounds 1-4 of Head. At the end of Round 4, there are 32 sc.
Round 5: Sc in each st around. (32 sc)
Round 6: Sc in each of next 8 sts, [sc-dec] 8 times, sc in each of next 8 sts. (24 sc)
Round 7: Sc in each st around. (24 sc)
Round 8: Sc in each of next 6 sts, [sc in next st, sc-dec] 4 times, sc in each of next 6 sts. (20 sc) Change to MC. Leave Color A hanging on the outside (image 5).

Round 9: Working in BLO, sc in each st around. (20 sc)
Round 10: Sc in each st around. (20 sc) Fasten off.

> » *Mark the 13th st of Round 10 (on First Leg only - for Joining Legs).*

Leg Detail

Working in FLO of Round 8, insert hook in first st and pick up Color A (image 6), ch 1, sc in each st around; fasten off with invisible join. (20 sc) (image 7).

Second Leg

Rounds 1-10: Repeat Rounds 1-10 of First Leg. At the end of Round 10, there are 20 sc.
Round 11: Sc in each of next 8 sts. Leave remaining sts unworked. Do not fasten off.

> » Repeat Leg Detail on Second Leg.

BODY

Round 1: *(Joining Legs)* Working on Second Leg, ch 4 (image 8); working on First Leg, sc in marked st (image 9), sc in each of next 19 sts; working in ch-4, sc in each of next 4 ch; working on Second Leg, sc in each of next 20 sts; working in unused loops on other side of ch-4, sc in each of next 4 ch. (48 sc) Mark last st made. Move marker each round.
Round 2: [Sc in each of next 7 sts, inc in next st] 6 times. (54 sc)
Round 3: Sc in each st around. (54 sc)
Round 4: Sc in each of next 43 sts, [inc in next st, sc in each of next 2 sts] 3 times, inc in next st, sc in next st. (58 sc)

Round 5: Sc in next st, inc in next st, sc in each of next 2 sts, inc in next st, sc in each of next 53 sts. (60 sc)

Round 6: Sc in each of next 13 sts, change to Color C, move marker to the last st made *(new end of round)*; sc in each of next 60 sts. (60 sc)

Round 7: Working in BLO, sc in each st around, change to Color D. (60 sc)

Alternate Color D and Color C every two rounds.

Rounds 8-10: *(3 Rounds)* Sc in each st around. (60 sc)

» Start stuffing Legs and Body firmly, adding more as you go.

Round 11 [Sc in each of next 8 sts, sc-dec] 6 times. (54 sc)

Rounds 12-14: *(3 Rounds)* Sc in each st around. (54 sc)

Round 15: [Sc in each of next 7 sts, sc-dec] 6 times. (48 sc)

Rounds 16-20: *(5 Rounds)* Sc in each st around. (48 sc)

Round 21: [Sc in each of next 6 sts, sc-dec] 6 times. (42 sc)

Rounds 22-24: *(3 Rounds)* Sc in each st around. (42 sc)

Round 25: [Sc in each of next 5 sts, sc-dec] 6 times. (36 sc)

Round 26 Sc in each st around. (36 sc)

Round 27 [Sc in each of next 4 sts, sc-dec] 6 times. (30 sc) Sl st in next st. Fasten off, leaving a long tail of Color C for sewing.

Sweater Detail

With feet facing upwards, working in FLO of Round 6, attach Color C to first st (image 10), ch 1, sc in each st around; fasten off with invisible join. (60 sc) (image 11).

HAT

Rounds 1-5: Using Red, repeat Rounds 1-5 of Head. At the end of Round 5, there are 40 sc.

Round 6: [Sc-dec] 17 times; working in FLO, sc in next st, hdc in next st, 2 dc in each of next 2 sts, hdc in next st, sc in next st. (25 sts) Sl st in next st. Fasten off, leaving a long tail for sewing.

» Sew Button to crown of Hat.

COLLAR

Row 1: *(Right Side)* Using Color D, ch 42, starting in third ch from hook, hdc in each ch across. (40 hdc)

Rows 2-3: *(2 Rows)* Ch 2, turn, hdc in each st across. (40 hdc) Fasten off, leaving a long tail for sewing.

Collar Detail

With Right Side facing, using Color C, work **surface slip stitches** across Row 2. Fasten off and weave in ends (images 12 &13).

NECK TIE

Using Red, ch 17, starting in third ch from hook, hdc in each ch across. (15 hdc) Fasten off, leaving a long tail for sewing.

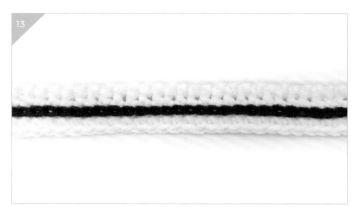

ASSEMBLY (use photos as guide)

Ears - Position Ears on either side of Head (between Rounds 4 & 19) and sew in place (image 14).

Nose - Position Nose between the Eyes and sew in place.

Eyebrows - Using Color A, embroider a straight stitch, two rounds above each Eye (image 15)

Arms - Position the Arms on either side of the Body (2 rounds below the last round of Body). Using long tails and yarn needle, sew them in place.

Head - Sew the Head to Body, stuffing firmly before closing.

Collar & Neck Tie - Position and sew Collar around neck (image 16). Fold the Neck Tie and sew it to the front of the Collar (images 17 & 18).

Hat - Position and sew the Hat on Head (image 19).

Face - Using a small makeup brush, apply blusher to the cheeks.

Little Panda Peter

Peter is only four months old, and the cutest baby panda ever! He loves playing hide-and-seek with his friends in the forest. When it is his turn to hide, he climbs a tree and puts leaves on his head to disguise himself so his friends can't see him.

MATERIALS

Scheepjes Softfun

Main Color (MC): White (2412)
Color A: Black Grey (2532)
Dark Green (2535) & Forest Green (2605) - small amounts for Leaves
Red (2410) & Forest Green (2605) - small amounts for Bow Tie
Pink (2514) - small amount for Eye accent

Scheepjes Softfun Denim

Color B: Yellow (520)

Scheepjes Maxi Sweet Treat (Cotton Thread)

Black (110) - for Nose

Size C-2 (2.75 mm) Crochet Hook - or size suitable for yarn used.
Yarn Needle
Embroidery Needle
Stitch Markers
⁵⁄₁₆" (8 mm) Safety Eyes - 2
Small Buttons - 2 - for Straps
Thread and needle - for sewing on buttons
Toy Stuffing

Finished Size
About 5½" (14 cm) tall

Skill Level

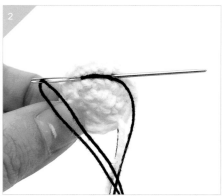
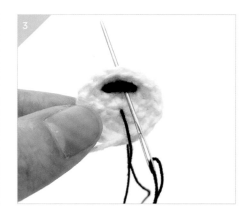

LEG (Make 2)

Round 1: Using Color A, make a Magic Ring; ch 1, 8 sc in ring, DO NOT JOIN. (8 sc) Tug tail to tighten ring. Mark last stitch.

Round 2: Inc in each st around. (16 sc) Move marker each round.

Round 3: Sc in next st, inc in next st, sc in each of next 4 sts, inc in each of next 4 sts, sc in each of next 4 sts, inc in next st, sc in next st. (22 sc)

Round 4: Sc in each st around. (22 sc)

Round 5: Sc in each of next 7 sts, [**sc-dec**] 4 times, sc in each of next 7 sts. (18 sc)

Round 6: Sc in each of next 5 sts, sc-dec, sc in each of next 4 sts, sc-dec, sc in each of next 5 sts. (16 sc)

Round 7: Sc in each of next 7 sts, sc-dec, sc in each of next 7 sts. (15 sc) Change to Color B.

Round 8: Sc in each of next 7 sts, inc in next st, sc in each of next 7 sts. (16 sc)

Round 9: Sc in each st around. (16 sc)

» Stuff Leg.

Last Row: Flatten the last round and working through both thicknesses, sc in each of next 8 sc.
Fasten off, leaving a long tail for sewing.

ARM (Make 2)

Round 1: Using Color A, make a Magic Ring; ch 1, 6 sc in ring, DO NOT JOIN. (6 sc) Tug tail to tighten ring. Mark last stitch.

Round 2: Inc in each st around. (12 sc) Move marker each round.

Rounds 3-10: *(8 Rounds)* Sc in each st around. (12 sc)

Round 11: [Sc in each of next 2 sts, sc-dec] 3 times. (9 sc)

» Stuff Arm lightly.

Last Row: Flatten the last round and working through both thicknesses, sc in each of next 4 sc. Fasten off, leaving a long tail for sewing.

EAR (Make 2)

Rounds 1-2: Using Color A, repeat Rounds 1-2 of Arm. At the end of Round 2, there are 12 sc.

Round 3: [Sc in each of next 2 sts, inc in next st] 4 times. (16 sc)

Round 4: Sc in each st around. (16 sc)

Round 5: [Sc in each of next 2 sts, sc-dec] 4 times. (12 sc) Sl st in next st. Fasten off, leaving a long tail for sewing.

TAIL

Rounds 1-5: Using Color A, repeat Rounds 1-5 of Ear. At the end of Round 5, there are 12 sc.

» Stuff Tail lightly.

Round 6: [Sc in next st, sc-dec] 4 times. (8 sc) Sl st in next st. Fasten off, leaving a long tail for sewing.

SNOUT

Rounds 1-2: Using MC, repeat Rounds 1-2 of Arm. At the end of Round 2, there are 12 sc.

Round 3: Sc in each of next 2 sts, inc in each of next 2 sts, sc in each of next 4 st, inc in each of next 2 sts, sc in each of next 2 sts. (16 sc) Sl st in next st. Fasten off, leaving a long tail for sewing.

» Using Cotton Thread and ebroidery needle, embroider a nose on Snout (images 2, 3 & 4).

HEAD & BODY

Note: *The colored font indicates where Color A is used. Use the Cut & Tie Method for the color changes.*

Rounds 1-2: Starting at Head, using MC, repeat Rounds 1-2 of Leg. At the end of Round 2, there are 16 sc.

Round 3: [Sc in next st, inc in next st] 8 times. (24 sc)

Round 4: [Sc in each of next 2 sts, inc in next st] 8 times. (32 sc)

Round 5: Sc in next st, inc in next st, [sc in each of next 3 sts, inc in next st] 7 times, sc in each of next 2 sts. (40 sc)

Round 6: [Sc in each of next 4 sts, inc in next st] 8 times. (48 sc)

Rounds 7-10: *(4 Rounds)* Sc in each st around. (48 sc)

Round 11: [Sc in each of next 7 sts, inc in next st] 6 times. (54 sc)

Round 12: Sc in each st around. (54 sc)

Round 13. Sc in each of next 5 sts; change to Color A, sc in each of next 3 sts; change to MC, sc in each of next 7 sts; change to Color A, sc in each of next 3 sts; change to MC, sc in each of next 36 sts. (54 sc)

Round 14: Sc in each of next 4 sts; change to Color A, sc in each of next 5 sts; change to MC, sc in each of next 5 sts; change to Color A, sc in each of next 5 sts; change to MC, sc in each of next 35 sts. (54 sc)

Round 15: Sc in each of next 3 sts; change to Color A, inc in next st, sc in each of next 15 sts, inc in next st; change to MC, sc in each of next 5 sts, [inc in next st, sc in each of next 8 sts] 3 times, inc in next st, sc in next st. (60 sc)

Rounds 16-17: *(2 Rounds)* Sc in each of next 3 sts; change to Color A, sc in each of next 19 sts; change to MC, sc in each of next 38 sts. (60 sc)

Round 18: Sc in each of next 5 sts; change to Color A, sc in each of next 2 sts, sc-dec, sc in next st; change to MC, sc in each of next 6 sts; change to Color A, sc in each of next 2 sts, sc-dec, sc in next st; change to MC, sc in each of next 7 sts, sc-dec, [sc in each of next 8 sts, sc-dec] 3 times. (54 sc) Fasten off Color A.

Round 19: Sc in each of next 3 sts, sc-dec, [sc in each of next 7 sts, sc-dec] 5 times, sc in each of next 4 sts. (48 sc)

Round 20: [Sc in each of next 6 sts, sc-dec] 6 times. (42 sc)

Round 21: Sc in each of next 2 sts, sc-dec, [sc in each of next 5 sts, sc-dec] 5 times, sc in each of next 3 sts. (36 sc)

Round 22: [Sc in each of next 4 sts, sc-dec] 6 times. (30 sc)

Round 23: [Sc in each of next 3 sts, sc-dec] 6 times, change to Color A. (24 sc)

» Insert Safety Eyes between Rounds 15 & 16, about 11 stitches apart.

» Using Pink, embroider a line below each Eye using straight stitch.

» Stuff Head firmly, adding more to Body as you go.

Round 24: [Sc in each of next 2 sts, inc in next st] 8 times. (32 sc)

Rounds 25-26: *(2 Rounds)* Sc in each st around. (32 sc)

Round 27: [Sc in each of next 3 sts, inc in next st] 8 times. (40 sc)

Round 28: Sc in each st around, change to MC. Fasten off Color A. (40 sc)

Round 29: Sc in each st around. (40 sc)

Round 30: [Sc in each of next 4 sts, inc in next st] 8 times. (48 sc)

Round 31: Sc in each st around, change to Color B. Fasten off MC. (48 sc)

Round 32: Sc in each st around. (48 sc)

Round 33: Working in BLO, [sc in each of next 11 sts, inc in next st] 4 times. (52 sc)

Round 34: Sc in each st around. (52 sc)

Round 35: [Sc in each of next 12 sts, inc in next st] 4 times. (56 sc)

Rounds 36-37: *(2 Rounds)* Sc in each st around. (56 sc)

Round 38: [Sc in each of next 5 sts, sc-dec] 8 times. (48 sc)

Round 39: Sc in each st around. (48 sc)

Round 40: [Sc in each of next 4 sts, sc-dec] 8 times. (40 sc)

Round 41: [Sc in each of next 3 sts, sc-dec] 8 times. (32 sc)

Round 42: [Sc in each of next 2 sts, sc-dec] 8 times. (24 sc)

Round 43: [Sc in next st, sc-dec] 8 times. (16 sc)

Round 44: [Sc-dec] 8 times. (8 sc)

» Finish stuffing Body.

Fasten off and close remaining sts, weaving in end (image 5).

PANTS DETAIL & STRAP

With Head facing down, on the FLO of Round 32, use pins to mark the 10 sts at center back (image 6). Attach Color B to first marked st, ch 30 (image 7), starting in the second ch from hook, sl st in each ch across (First Strap made - photo 8); working on Body, sl st in each st across to next marked st; ch 30 (image 9), starting in the second ch from hook, sl st in each ch across (Second Strap made); working on Body (image 10), sl st in each remaining st around. Fasten off, leaving a long tail for sewing Straps to Body.

ASSEMBLY - Use photos as guide

Ears - Position Ears on either side of Head (between Rounds 6 & 9) and sew in place (images 12 & 13).

Snout - Sew Snout on Head, between Eyes (image 14).

Arms - Position Arms on either side of Body (1 round below Neck). Using long tails and yarn needle, sew them in place.

Straps - Cross the straps at the back (image 15) and pin the ends of Straps in position on the front of the Body. Using long tail from Pants Detail, insert needle through Body to front (image 16) and sew Straps in place (image 17). Sew a small button on each Strap (images 18).

Legs - Position and sew Legs on either side of Body, 2 rounds below Pants Detail (between Rounds 35 & 41) (images 19 & 20).

Tail - Position and sew Tail to center back of Body (between Rounds 37 & 38) (image 21).

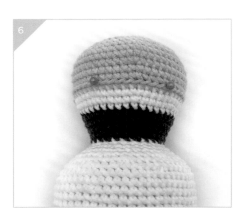

ACCESSORIES

(image 11 - Bow Tie & Leaves)

Bow Tie

Using Red, ch 7, starting in the third ch from the hook, dc in each ch across. (5 dc) Fasten off and weave in ends.

» Wrap a small length of Forest Green tightly around the center of the Bow Tie. Secure and leave a long tail for sewing.

» Using tail, sew Bow Tie below Neck.

Leaf (Make 2 - one in each color)

Using Leaf Color, ch 6, starting in the second ch from hook, sc in each of next 2 ch, hdc in next ch, sc in next ch, (sc, ch 2, sc) in the last ch; working in unused loops on other side of starting ch, sc in next ch, hdc in next ch, sc in each of next 2 ch; join with sl st to first sc; ch 2. Fasten off, leaving a long tail for sewing.

» Position and sew Leaves to top of Head (image 22).

Little Bunny Suzy

Little Suzy is an avid gardener and loves tending her carrot patch. Today she pulled up the most beautiful, big carrot. She's rushing home with it so her mother can bake a delicious carrot cake for the Bunny family.

MATERIALS

Scheepjes Softfun

Main Color (MC): White (2412)
Color A: Light Pink (2513)
Color B: Rose Pink (2608)
Orange (2427) & Forest Green (2605) - small amount for Carrot

Scheepjes Maxi Sweet Treat (Cotton Thread)

Black Coffee (162) - for Carrot detail

Size C-2 (2.75 mm) Crochet Hook - or size suitable for yarn used.
Yarn Needle
Ebroidery Needle
Stitch Markers
⁵⁄₁₆" (8 mm) Safety Eyes - 2
Toy Stuffing
Cosmetic Blusher & Brush - for Cheeks

Finished Size
About 6¼" (16 cm) tall

Skill Level
♥

ARM (Make 2)

(image 1 - Arms, Legs & Ears)

Round 1: Using MC, make a Magic Ring; ch 1, 8 sc in ring, DO NOT JOIN. (8 sc) Tug tail to tighten ring. Mark last stitch.
Round 2: [**Inc** in next st, sc in next st] 4 times. (12 sc) Move marker each round.
Rounds 3-6: *(4 Rounds)* Sc in each st around. (12 sc)
Round 7: [Sc in next st, **sc-dec**] 4 times. (8 sc)
Round 8: Sc in each st around. (8 sc)

» Stuff Arm lightly.

Last Row: Flatten the last round and working through both thicknesses, sc in each of next 4 sc. Fasten off, leaving a long tail for sewing.

LEG (Make 2)

Round 1: Using MC, make a Magic Ring; ch 1, 8 sc in ring, DO NOT JOIN. (8 sc) Tug tail to tighten ring. Mark last stitch.
Round 2: Inc in each st around. (16 sc) Move marker each round.
Round 3: Sc in next st, inc in next st, sc in each of next 5 sts, inc in each of next 2 sts, sc in each of next 5 sts, inc in next st, sc in next st. (20 sc)
Round 4: Sc in each st around. (20 sc)
Round 5: Sc in each of next 6 sts, [sc-dec] 4 times, sc in each of next 6 sts. (16 sc)
Round 6: [Sc in each of next 4 sts, sc-dec] 2 times, sc in each of next 4 sts. (14 sc)
Round 7: Sc in each of next 6 sts, sc-dec, sc in each of next 6 sts. (13 sc)
Round 8: Sc in each of next 6 sts, inc in next st, sc in each of next 6 sts. (14 sc)

» Stuff Leg.

Last Row: Flatten the last round and working through both thicknesses, sc in each of next 7 sc. Fasten off, leaving a long tail for sewing.

EAR (Make 2)

Note: *The colored font indicates where Color A is used. Use the Stranding Method for the color changes.*

Rounds 1-2: Using MC, repeat Rounds 1-2 of Leg. At the end of Round 2, there are 16 sc.
Rounds 3-4: *(2 Rounds)* Sc in each st around. (16 sc)
Round 5: Sc in each of next 7 sts; change to Color A, sc in each of next 2 sts; change to MC, sc in each of next 7 sts. (16 sc)
Rounds 6-7: *(2 Rounds)* Sc in each of next 6 sts; change to Color A, sc in each of next 4 sts; change to MC, sc in each of next 6 sts. (16 sc)

Round 8: Sc in each of next 4 sts, sc-dec; change to Color A, sc in each of next 4 sts; change to MC, sc-dec, sc in each of next 4 sts. (14 sc)
Rounds 9-11: *(3 Rounds)* Sc in each of next 5 sts; change to Color A, sc in each of next 4 sts; change to MC, sc in each of next 5 sts. (14 sc) Fasten off Color A.
Round 12: Sc in each of next 3 sts, sc-dec, sc in each of next 4 sts, sc-dec, sc in each of next 3 sts. (12 sc) Sl st in next st. Fasten off, leaving a long tail for sewing.

TAIL

Rounds 1-2: Using MC, repeat Rounds 1-2 of Leg. At the end of Round 2, there are 16 sc.
Round 3: [Sc in each of next 3 sts, inc in next st] 4 times. (20 sc)
Rounds 4-5: *(2 Rounds)* Sc in each st around. (20 sc)
Round 6: [Sc in each of next 3 sts, sc-dec] 4 times. (16 sc)

» Stuff Tail lightly.

Round 7: [Sc-dec] 8 times. (8 sc) Sl st in next st. Fasten off, leaving a long tail for sewing.

HEAD & BODY

Rounds 1-2: Starting at Head, using MC, repeat Rounds 1-2 of Leg. At the end of Round 2, there are 16 sc.
Round 3: [Sc in next st, inc in next st] 8 times. (24 sc)
Round 4: [Sc in each of next 2 sts, inc in next st] 8 times. (32 sc)
Round 5: Sc in next st, inc in next st, [sc in each of next 3 sts, inc in next st] 7 times, sc in each of next 2 sts. (40 sc)
Round 6: [Sc in each of next 4 sts, inc in next st] 8 times. (48 sc)
Rounds 7-10: *(4 Rounds)* Sc in each st around. (48 sc)
Round 11: [Sc in each of next 7 sts, inc in next st] 6 times. (54 sc)
Rounds 12-15: *(4 Rounds)* Sc in each st around. (54 sc)
Round 16: [Sc in each of next 8 sts, inc in next st] 6 times. (60 sc)
Round 17: Sc in each st around. (60 sc)
Round 18: [Sc in each of next 8 sts, sc-dec] 6 times. (54 sc)
Round 19: Sc in each of next 3 sts, sc-dec, [sc in each of next 7 sts, sc-dec] 5 times, sc in each of next 4 sts. (48 sc)
Round 20: [Sc in each of next 6 sts, sc-dec] 6 times. (42 sc)
Round 21: Sc in each of next 2 sts, sc-dec, [sc in each of next 5 sts, sc-dec] 5 times, sc in each of next 3 sts. (36 sc)
Round 22: [Sc in each of next 4 sts, sc-dec] 6 times. (30 sc)
Round 23: [Sc in each of next 3 sts, sc-dec] 6 times, change to Color A. (24 sc) Fasten off MC.

» Insert Safety Eyes between Rounds 15 & 16, about 9 stitches apart.

» Stuff Head firmly, adding more to Body as you go.

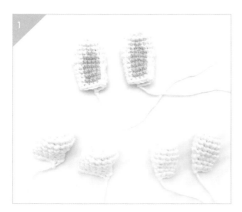

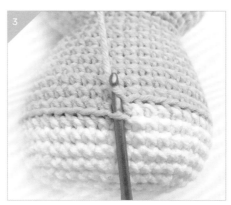

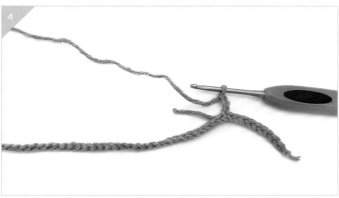

Round 24: [Sc in each of next 2 sts, inc in next st] 8 times. (32 sc)

Rounds 25-26: *(2 Rounds)* Sc in each st around. (32 sc)

Round 27: [Sc in each of next 3 sts, inc in next st] 8 times. (40 sc)

Rounds 28-29: *(2 Rounds)* Sc in each st around. (40 sc)

Round 30: [Sc in each of next 4 sts, inc in next st] 8 times. (48 sc)

Rounds 31-32: *(2 Rounds)* Sc in each st around. (48 sc)

Round 33: [Sc in each of next 11 sts, inc in next st] 4 times. (52 sc)

Round 34: Sc in each st around, change to MC. (52 sc) Leave Color A hanging on the outside (image 2).

Round 35: Working in BLO, [sc in each of next 12 sts, inc in next st] 4 times. (56 sc)

Rounds 36-37: *(2 Rounds)* Sc in each st around. (56 sc)

Round 38: [Sc in each of next 5 sts, sc-dec] 8 times. (48 sc)

Round 39: Sc in each st around. (48 sc)

Round 40: [Sc in each of next 4 sts, sc-dec] 8 times. (40 sc)

Round 41: [Sc in each of next 3 sts, sc-dec] 8 times. (32 sc)

Round 42: [Sc in each of next 2 sts, sc-dec] 8 times. (24 sc)

Round 43: [Sc in next st, sc-dec] 8 times. (16 sc)

Round 44: [Sc-dec] 8 times. (8 sc)

» Finish stuffing Body.

Fasten off and close remaining sts, weaving in end.

Sweater Detail: Working in FLO of Round 34, insert hook in first st and pick up Color A (image 3), sl st in each st around. Fasten off and weave in ends.

BOW

Row 1: (Wrong Side) Using Color B, ch 7, starting in the third ch from the hook, dc in each ch across. (5 dc)

Rows 2-4: *(3 Rows)* Ch 3, turn, dc in each st across. (5 dc) At the end of Row 4, fasten off and weave in ends.

» Wrap a small length of Color A tightly around the center of the Bow - between 2nd and 3rd Rows. Secure and leave a long tail for sewing.

COLLAR

Using Color B, ch 50. Fasten off.

Attach yarn to the 11th ch from the end (40th ch from beginning) (image 4), ch 3, 2 dc in same st as joining, 3 dc in each of next 29 ch. (90 dc) Leave remaining 10 ch unworked. Fasten off and weave in ends (image 5).

ASSEMBLY (use photos as guide)

Nose – Using Color A, embroider a Nose (over 3 sts) between the Eyes using straight stitches.

Ears – Position Ears on either side of Head, between Rounds 5 & 7, and sew in place (image 6).

Bow – Sew on Head (image 7).

Sweater – Using Color B, embroider some hearts ("V"s) on front of Body (image 8)

Legs – Position the Legs on either side of the Body (below the Sweater Detail). Using long tails and yarn needle, sew them in place (image 9).

Collar – Wrap Collar around Neck and tie in front.

Arms – Position the Arms on either side of the Body (3 rounds below Neck). Using long tails and yarn needle, sew them in place (images 10 & 11).

Tail – Sew Tail to center back of Body (image 12).

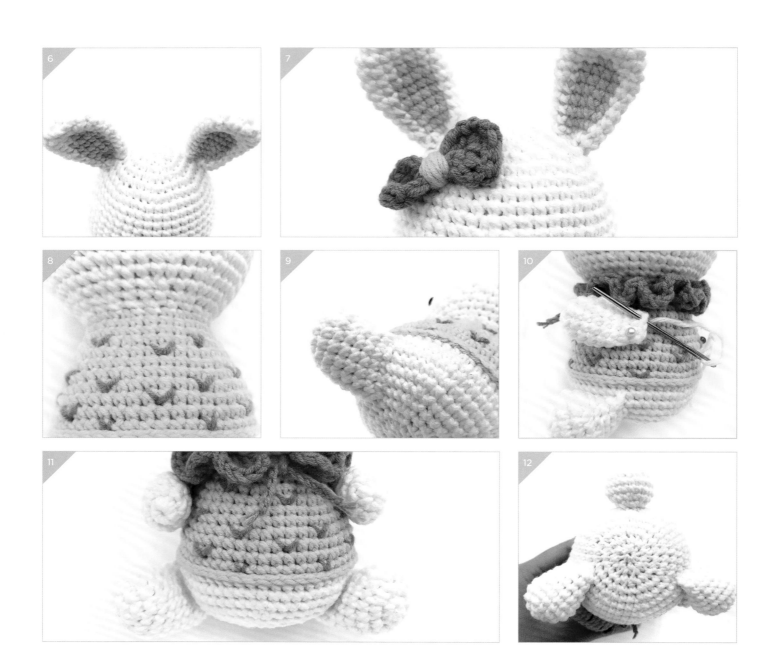

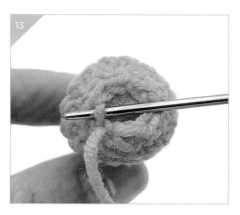  

CARROT

Round 1: Using Orange, make a Magic Ring; ch 1, 6 sc in ring, DO NOT JOIN. (6 sc) Tug tail to tighten ring. Mark last stitch.

Round 2: [Inc in next st, sc in next st] 3 times. (9 sc) Move marker each round.

Round 3: Sc in each st around. (9 sc)

Round 4: [Sc in each of next 2 sts, inc in next st] 3 times. (12 sc)

Rounds 5-6: *(2 Rounds)* Sc in each st around. (12 sc)

Round 7: [Sc in each of next 2 sts, inc in next st] 4 times. (16 sc)

Rounds 8-9: *(2 Rounds)* Sc in each st around. (16 sc)

» Stuff Carrot.

Round 10: [Sc-dec] 8 times. (8 sc) Fasten off and working in BLO (from inside to outside), close remaining sts (image 13) and secure, threading the tail through the carrot for sewing (image 14).

Carrot Leaves - Working in FLO of Round 10"(Working in FLO of Round 10) (image 15), attach Forest Green to last st (image 16), *sl st in next st; ch 4, starting in the second ch from hook, sl st in each of 3 ch across; working in Carrot, sl st in next st; repeat from * 3 times more. Fasten off and weave in ends (image 17).

» Using Cotton Thread, embroider some small lines using straight stitch on Carrot (image 18).

» Using long tail, sew it to the Body, near an arm.

Little April

When Little April awoke this morning, there was a wrapped gift from her mother on the bedside table. Inside was a beautiful new bow! She loves it so much, she's going to wear it today, with her favorite lemon dress. Thank you, Mommy!

MATERIALS

Scheepjes Catona

Main Color (MC): Bridal White (105)
Color A: Lemon (280)
Color B: Lemon Chiffon (100)
Color C: Green Yellow (245)
Kiwi (205), Powder Pink (238) & Baby Blue (509) - small amounts for Flowers

Scheepjes Softfun

Brown (2623) - for Hair

Scheepjes Maxi Sweet Treat (Cotton Thread)

Black Coffee (162) - for Eyelashes & Eyebrows

Sizes B-1 (2.25 mm) (Main Hook) & C-2 (2.75 mm) Crochet Hooks - or sizes suitable for yarn used. (Use Main Hook throughout, unless otherwise stated.)
Yarn Needle
Ebroidery Needle
Stitch Markers
5⁄16" (8 mm) Safety Eyes - 2
Small Beads or Buttons - 2
Lacy Ribbon - ¾" (3 cm) wide and 4" (10 cm) long
Thread and needle - for sewing on Beads / Buttons and Ribbon
Toy Stuffing
Cosmetic Blusher & Brush - for Cheeks

Finished Size
About 8½" (22 cm) tall

Skill Level
♥♥

HEAD

Round 1: Using MC, make a Magic Ring; ch 1, 8 sc in ring, DO NOT JOIN. (8 sc) Tug tail to tighten ring.
Mark last stitch.
Round 2: Inc in each st around. (16 sc) Move marker each round.
Round 3: [Sc in next st, inc in next st] 8 times. (24 sc)
Round 4: [Sc in each of next 2 sts, inc in next st] 8 times. (32 sc)
Round 5 [Sc in each of next 3 sts, inc in next st] 8 times. (40 sc)
Round 6 [Sc in each of next 4 sts, inc in next st] 8 times. (48 sc)
Rounds 7-10: *(4 Rounds)* Sc in each st around. (48 sc)
Round 11: [Sc in each of next 7 sts, inc in next st] 6 times. (54 sc)
Rounds 12-16: *(4 Rounds)* Sc in each st around. (54 sc)
Round 17: [Sc in each of next 8 sts, inc in next st] 6 times. (60 sc)
Round 18: [Sc in each of next 8 sts, **sc-dec**] 6 times. (54 sc)
Round 19: Sc in each of next 3 sts, sc-dec, [sc in each of next 7 sts, sc-dec] 5 times, sc in each of next 4 sts. (48 sc)
Round 20: [Sc in each of next 6 sts, sc-dec] 6 times. (42 sc)
Round 21: Sc in each of next 2 sts, sc-dec, [sc in each of next 5 sts, sc-dec] 5 times, sc in each of next 3 sts. (36 sc)
Round 22: [Sc in each of next 4 sts, sc-dec] 6 times. (30 sc)

» Insert Safety Eyes between Rounds 14 & 15, about 9 stitches apart.

» Stuff Head firmly, adding more as you go.

Round 23: Sc in next st, sc-dec, [sc in each of next 3 sts, sc-dec] 5 times, sc in each of next 2 sts. (24 sc)
Round 24: [Sc in each of next 2 sts, sc-dec] 6 times. (18 sc)
Sl st in next st. Fasten off, leaving a long tail for sewing.

» Using Cotton Thread, embroider an Eyebrow (2 rounds above Eye), and an Eyelash for each Eye (images 1 & 2).

ARM (Make 2)

Note: *Arms are not stuffed.*

Round 1: Using MC, make a Magic Ring; ch 1, 8 sc in ring, DO NOT JOIN. (8 sc) Tug tail to tighten ring.
Mark last stitch, move the marker each round.
Rounds 2-11: *(10 Rounds)* Sc in each st around. (8 sc) At the end of Round 11, change to Color A. Fasten off MC
Round 12: Working in BLO, [sc in next st, inc in next st] 4 times. (12 sc)
Rounds 13-15: *(3 Rounds)* Sc in each st around. (12 sc)
Round 16: [Sc in each of next 2 sts, sc-dec] 3 times. (9 sc)
Round 17: [Sc in next st, sc-dec] 3 times. (6 sc)

Last Row: Flatten the last round and working through both thicknesses, sc in each of next 3 sc.
Fasten off, leaving a long tail for sewing.

Arm Detail

Working in FLO of Round 11, attach Color B to any st, [ch 3, sl st in next st] 8 times. Fasten off and weave in ends (image 3).

LEGS

First Leg

Rounds 1-2: Using Color C, repeat Rounds 1-2 of Head. At the end of Round 2, there are 16 sc.
Round 3: Sc in next st, inc in next st, sc in each of next 4 sts, inc in each of next 4 sts, sc in each of next 4 sts, inc in next st, sc in last st. (22 sc)
Rounds 4-6: *(3 Rounds)* Sc in each st around. (22 sc)
At the end of Round 6, change to Color B. Leave Color C hanging on the outside.
Round 7: Working in BLO, sc in each of next 7 sts, [sc-dec] 4 times, sc in each of next 7 sts (18 sc)
Round 8: Sc in each st around. (18 sc)
Round 9: Sc in each of next 5 sts, [sc-dec] 4 times, sc in each of next 5 sts (14 sc)

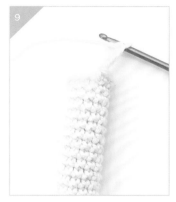

Rounds 10-12: *(3 Rounds)* Sc in each st around. (14 sc) At the end of the Round 12, change to MC. Leave Color B hanging on the outside (image 4).

» Start stuffing Leg firmly, adding more as you go.

Round 13: Working in BLO, [sc in each of next 5 sts, sc-dec] 2 times. (12 sc)

Note: *I prefer to work the Foot Detail at this point, before continuing with the Leg.*

Rounds 14-26: *(13 Rounds)* Sc in each st around. (12 sc) At the end of Round 26, change to Color B. Fasten off MC.

Round 27: Sc in each st around. (12 sc)

Round 28: Sc in each of next 11 sts. (11 sc) Leave remaining st unworked. Fasten off.

Foot Detail

Sock Frill: Working in FLO of Round 12, insert hook in first st and pick up Color B, [ch 2, sl st in next st] 14 times. Fasten off and weave in end (image 5).

Shoe Detail & Strap: Working in FLO of Round 6, insert hook in first st and pick up Color C, ch 1, sc in each of next 7 sts, [sc-dec] 4 times, sc in each of next 7 sts; join with sl st to first sc; ch 15. Fasten off, leaving a long tail for sewing (image 6).

» Wrap the ch-15 Strap around the Leg, and using the tail, sew to the last st of Round 6 (images 7 & 8).

Second Leg

Rounds 1-27: Repeat Rounds 1-27 of First Leg. At the end of Round 27, there are 12 sc.

» Repeat Foot Detail on Second Leg.

Round 28: Sc in each of next 7 sts. Leave remaining sts unworked. Do not fasten off.

BODY

Round 1: *(Joining Legs)* Working on Second Leg, ch 4 (image 9); working on First Leg, sc in last st made (image 10), sc in each of next 11 sts; working in ch-4, sc in each of next 4 ch; working on Second Leg, sc in each of next 12 sts; working in unused loops on other side of ch-4, sc in each of next 4 ch. (32 sc) Mark last st made. Move marker each round.

Round 2: [Sc in each of next 12 sts, inc in next st, sc in each of next 2 sts, inc in next st] 2 times. (36 sc)

Rounds 3-8: *(6 Rounds)* Sc in each st around. (36 sc)

Round 9: [Sc in each of next 4 sts, sc-dec] 6 times. (30 sc)

» Start stuffing Body, adding more as you go.

Rounds 10-15: *(6 Rounds)* Sc in each st around. (30 sc)

Round 16: Working in BLO, [sc in each of next 3 sts, sc-dec] 6 times. (24 sc)

Round 17: Working in BLO, sc in each st around. (24 sc)

Round 18: [Sc in each of next 2 sts, sc-dec] 6 times. (18 sc) Sl st in next st. Fasten off, leaving a long tail for sewing.

DRESS

Round 1: With Legs facing upwards, working in FLO of Round 15 of Body, attach Color A to the last st worked (image 11), ch 1, sc in each st around. (30 sc) DO NOT JOIN.

Rounds 2-6: *(5 Rounds)* Sc in each st around. (30 sc)

Round 7: [Sc in each of next 4 sts, inc in next st] 6 times. (36 sc)

Rounds 8-9: *(2 Rounds)* Sc in each st around. (36 sc)

Round 10: [Sc in each of next 5 sts, inc in next st] 6 times. (42 sc)

Rounds 11-13: *(3 Rounds)* Sc in each st around. (42 sc)

Round 14: [Sc in each of next 6 sts, inc in next st] 6 times. (48 sc)

Rounds 15-19: *(5 Rounds)* Sc in each st around. (48 sc)

Round 20: [Sc in each of next 7 sts, inc in next st] 6 times. (54 sc)

Rounds 21-22: *(2 Rounds)* Sc in each st around. (54 sc). Fasten off with invisible join.

COLLAR

Row 1: With Legs facing upwards, working in FLO of Round 16 of Body, attach Color C to the st at center front of Body (image 12), ch 1, sc in each of next 2 sts, inc in next st, [sc in each of next 3 sts, inc] 5 times, sc in next st. (30 sc)

Row 2: Ch 1, turn, sc in first st, hdc in next st, dc in each of next 26 sts, hdc in next st, sc in next st, change to Color B. (30 sts) Fasten off Color C.

Row 3: *(Ruffle)* Turn, [ch 4, sl st in next st] 30 times. Fasten off and weave in ends (image 13).

HAIR

Round 1: Using Brown, make a Magic Ring; ch 1, 6 sc in ring, DO NOT JOIN. (6 sc) Tug tail to tighten ring. Mark last stitch.

Round 2: Inc in each st around. (12 sc) Move marker each round.

Round 3: Working in BLO, [sc in next st, inc in next st] 6 times. (18 sc)

First Layer

Working in BLO of Round 3, *[sl st in next st; ch 45, starting in second ch from hook, sc in each ch across (44 sc); sl st in next st] 5 times, [sl st in next st; ch 15, starting in second ch from hook, sc in each ch across (14 sc); sl st in next st] 4 times*. (5 long strands & 4 shorter strands)

Second Layer

Working in FLO of Round 3 (image 14), repeat from * to * of First Layer.

Third Layer

Working in FLO of Round 2, [sl st in next st; ch 45, starting in second ch from hook, sc in each ch across (44 sc); sl st in next st] 6 times. (6 long strands) Fasten off, leaving a very long tail for sewing (image 15).

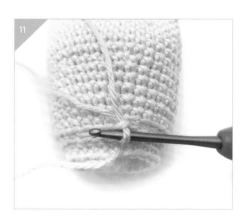

BOW

Using Lacy Ribbon (image 16), sew ends of Ribbon together to create a ring (image 17). Flatten the ring (with seam in center) and stitch (image 18).
Wind the thread tightly around the Ribbon, to create a Bow, and secure (image 19). Wrap a small length of Powder Pink around the center of the Bow (covering the thread). Secure and leave a long tail for sewing (image 20).

FLOWER (Make 3 - one in each color)

Make a Magic Ring; ch 1, 5 sc in ring; tug tail to tighten ring; join with sl st to first sc. (5 sc)
Fasten off, leaving a long tail for sewing.

ASSEMBLY (use photos as guide)

Arms - Position the Arms on either side of the Body, at about Round 3 of Dress. Using long tails and yarn needle, sew them in place, working through the Dress into the Body, to secure them.

Beads - Sew the beads/buttons on front of Dress.

Flowers - Position and sew the Flowers on one side of Dress (image 21).

Head - Sew Head to Body.

Hair - Place Hair on Head, using pins to keep it in place (images 22 & 23). Using the long tail and yarn needle, sew the strands in place.

Bow - Sew on Head.

Face - Using a small makeup brush, apply blusher to the cheeks.

Lulu Otter

Lulu is a happy little otter, who always has a smile for everyone. She's also very clever at catching fish! Her favorite pastime is lying on her back, floating down the river, eating her delicious lunch.

MATERIALS

Scheepjes Softfun

Main Color (MC): Light Peach (2466)
Color A: Cream (2426)
Brown (2623) - small amount for Eyes and Nose
Light Yellow (2496), Orange (2427) & Yellow (2518) - small amounts for Fish

Scheepjes Softfun Denim

Color B: Brown (510)

Scheepjes Catona

Kiwi (205) - small amount for Leaf

Scheepjes Maxi Sweet Treat (Cotton Thread)

Black Coffee (162) - for Whiskers

Size C-2 (2.75 mm) Crochet Hook - or size suitable for yarn used.
Yarn Needle
Embroidery Needle
Stitch Markers
Toy Stuffing
Cosmetic Blusher & Brush - for Cheeks

Finished Size
About 10 ⅝" (27 cm) tall

Skill Level
♥

71

HEAD & BODY

Note: *The colored font indicates where Color A is used. Use the Cut & Tie Method for the color changes.*

Round 1: Starting at Head, using MC, make a Magic Ring; ch 1, 8 sc in ring, DO NOT JOIN. (8 sc) Tug tail to tighten ring. Mark last st.

Round 2: Inc in each st around. (16 sc) Move marker each round.

Round 3: [Sc in next st, inc in next st] 8 times. (24 sc)

Round 4: [Sc in each of next 2 sts, inc in next st] 8 times. (32 sc)

Round 5: Sc in next st, inc in next st, [sc in each of next 3 sts, inc in next st] 7 times, sc in each of next 2 sts. (40 sc)

Round 6: [Sc in each of next 4 sts, inc in next st] 8 times. (48 sc)

Rounds 7-10: *(4 Rounds)* Sc in each st around. (48 sc)

Round 11: [Sc in each of next 7 sts, inc in next st] 6 times. (54 sc)

Rounds 12-14: *(3 Rounds)* Sc in each st around. (54 sc)

Rounds 15-16: *(2 Rounds)* Sc in each of next 27 sts; change to Color A, sc in each of next 27 sts, change to MC. (54 sc)

Round 17: [Sc in each of next 8 sts, inc in next st] 3 times; change to Color A, [sc in each of next 8 sts, inc in next st] 3 times, change to MC. (60 sc)

Round 18: [Sc in each of next 8 sts, **sc-dec**] 3 times; change to Color A, [sc in each of next 8 sts, sc-dec] 3 times, change to MC. (54 sc)

Round 19: Sc in each of next 3 sts, sc-dec, [sc in each of next 7 sts, sc-dec] 2 times, sc in each of next 4 sts; change co Color A, sc in each of next 3 sts, sc-dec, [sc in each of next 7 sts, sc-dec] 2 times, sc in each of next 4 sts, change to MC. (48 sc)

Round 20: [Sc in each of next 6 sts, sc-dec] 3 times; change to Color A, [sc in each of next 6 sts, sc-dec] 3 times, change to MC. (42 sc)

Round 21: Sc in each of next 2 sts, sc-dec, [sc in each of next 5 sts, sc-dec] 2 times, sc in each of next 3 sts; change to Color A, sc in each of next 2 sts, sc-dec, [sc in each of next 5 sts, sc-dec] 2 times, sc in each of next 3 sts, change to MC. (36 sc)

Round 22: [Sc in each of next 4 sts, sc-dec] 3 times; change to Color A, [sc in each of next 4 sts, sc-dec] 3 times, change to MC. (30 sc)

Round 23: [Sc in each of next 3 sts, sc-dec] 3 times; change to Color A, [sc in each of next 3 sts, sc-dec] 3 times, change to MC. (24 sc) Fasten off Color A.

» Start stuffing Head, adding more as you go.

Round 24: [Sc in each of next 3 sts, inc in next st] 6 times. (30 sc)

Round 25: [Sc in each of next 4 sts, inc in next st] 6 times. (36 sc)

Rounds 26-33: *(8 Rounds)* Sc in each st around. (36 sc)

Round 34: [Sc in each of next 5 sts, inc in next st] 6 times. (42 sc)

Round 35: [Sc in each of next 6 sts, inc in next st] 6 times. (48 sc)

Rounds 36-40: *(5 Rounds)* Sc in each st around. (48 sc)

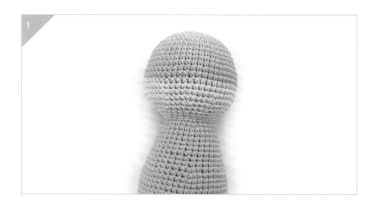

Round 41: [Sc in each of next 7 sts, inc in next st] 6 times. (54 sc)

Rounds 42-43: *(2 Rounds)* Sc in each st around. (54 sc)

Round 44: [Sc in each of next 7 sts, sc-dec] 6 times. (48 sc)

Round 45: Sc in each st around. (48 sc),

Round 46: [Sc in each of next 6 sts, sc-dec] 6 times. (42 sc)

Round 47: Sc in each of next 2 sts, sc-dec, [sc in each of next 5 sts, sc-dec] 5 times, sc in each of next 3 sts. (36 sc)

Round 48: [Sc in each of next 4 sts, sc-dec] 6 times. (30 sc)

Round 49: [Sc in each of next 3 sts, sc-dec] 6 times. (24 sc)

Round 50: [Sc in each of next 2 sts, sc-dec] 6 times. (18 sc)

Round 51 [Sc in next st, sc-dec] 6 times. (12 sc)

Round 52: [Sc-dec] 6 times. (6 sc)

» Finish stuffing Body.

Fasten off and close remaining sts, weaving in end (image 1).

Ears, Arms, Tail & Webbed Feet

EAR (Make 2)

Round 1: Using Color B, make a Magic Ring; ch 1, 6 sc in ring, DO NOT JOIN. (6 sc) Tug tail to tighten ring. Mark last st.

Round 2: Inc in each st around. (12 sc) Move marker each round.

Rounds 3-4: *(2 Rounds)* Sc in eachst around. (12 sc)
At the end of Round 4, sl st in next st.
Fasten off, leaving a long tail for sewing.

ARM (Make 2)

Round 1: Using Color B, make a Magic Ring; ch 1, 6 sc in ring, DO NOT JOIN. (6 sc) Tug tail to tighten ring. Mark last stitch.

Round 2: [Inc in next st, sc in each of next 2 sts] 2 times. (8 sc) Move marker each round.

Round 3: Sc in each of next 7 sts, inc in the last st. (9 sc)

Round 4: Sc in each of next 8 sts, inc in the last st. (10 sc)

Round 5: Sc in each of next 9 sts, inc in the last st. (11 sc)

Round 6: Sc in each of next 10 sts, inc in the last st. (12 sc)

Round 7: Sc in each of next 11 sts, inc in the last st. (13 sc)

Round 8: Sc in each of next 12 sts, inc in the last st. (14 sc)

Rounds 9-10: *(2 Rounds)* Sc in each st around. (14 sc)

» Stuff Arm lightly.

Round 11: [Sc-dec] 7 times. (7 sc) Fasten off and close remaining sts, leaving a long tail for sewing.

TAIL

Rounds 1-2: Using Color B, repeat Rounds 1-2 of Arm. At the end of Round 2, there are 8 sc.

Round 3: Sc in each st around. (8 sc)

Round 4: [Sc in each of next 3 sts, inc in next st] 2 times. (10 sc)

Round 5: Sc in each st around. (10 sc)

Round 6: [Sc in each of next 4 sts, inc in next st] 2 times. (12 sc)

Round 7: Sc in each st around. (12 sc)

Round 8: [Sc in each of next 5 sts, inc in next st] 2 times. (14 sc)

Rounds 9-10: *(2 Rounds)* Sc in each st around. (14 sc)

Round 11: [Sc in each of next 6 sts, inc in next st] 2 times. (16 sc)

Rounds 12-14: *(3 Rounds)* Sc in each st around. (16 sc)

Round 15: [Sc in each of next 7 sts, inc in next st] 2 times. (18 sc)

» Start stuffing Tail lightly, adding more as you go.

Rounds 16-18: *(3 Rounds)* Sc in each st around. (18 sc)

Round 19: [Sc in each of next 8 sts, inc in next st] 2 times. (20 sc)

Rounds 20-24: *(5 Rounds)* Sc in each st around. (20 sc)

Round 25: [Sc in each of next 9 sts, inc in next st] 2 times. (22 sc)

Rounds 26-29: *(4 Rounds)* Sc in each st around. (22 sc)

Last Row: Flatten the last round and working through both thicknesses, sc in each of next 11 sc. Fasten off, leaving a long tail for sewing.

WEBBED FOOT (Make 2)

Toes (Make 3)

Round 1: Using Color B, make a Magic Ring; ch 1, 6 sc in ring, DO NOT JOIN. (6 sc) Tug tail to tighten ring.

Round 2: Sc in each st around. (6 sc)

At the end of Round 2, for the first and second Toes, fasten off. For the third Toe, do not fasten off.

Foot

Round 1: *(Joining Toes)* Working on the first Toe, sc in last st made (image 2), sc in each of next 2 sts; working on second Toe, sc in last st made (image 3), sc in each of next 5 sts; working on first Toe, sc in each of remaining 3 sts; working on the third Toe, sc in each of next 6 sts. (18 sc) DO NOT JOIN. Mark last st made. Move marker each round.

Round 2: [Sc in next st, sc-dec] 6 times. (12 sc)

Rounds 3-6: *(4 Rounds)* Sc in each st around. (12 sc)

» Stuff foot lightly.

Round 7: [Sc-dec] 6 times. (6 sc) Fasten off and close remaining sts, leaving a long tail for sewing.

ASSEMBLY (use photos as guide)

Nose - Using Brown and yarn needle, embroider a Nose over 3 stitches, using straight stitches to center front of face (Color A section), between Rounds 14 & 15.

Eyes - Using Brown, embroider Smiling Eyes (over 4 sts and 2 rounds) starting between Rounds 13 & 14, about 7 sts between the Eyes (images 4, 5, 6, 7 & 8)

Whiskers - Using Cotton Thread, embroider whiskers using straight stitches, 2 rounds below each Eye (images 9, 10 & 11).

Ears - Position Ears on either side of Head (between Rounds 5 and 7). Using long tails and yarn needle, sew in place (images 12 & 13).

Arms - Position Arms on either side of the Body (2 rounds below Neck). Using long tails and yarn needle, sew them in place, tacking the Hands to Body (images 14, 15, 16 & 17).

Feet - Position the Feet on Body (about 8th round from last round). Using long tails and yarn needle, sew them in place, keeping the Toes free (images 18, 19 & 20).

Tail - Position the Tail at center back of Body (about 6th round from last round). Using long tails and yarn needle, sew it in place (images 21, 22 & 23).

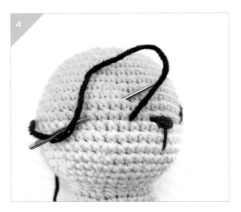
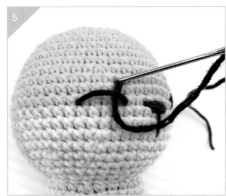

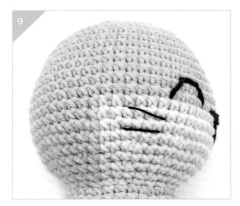
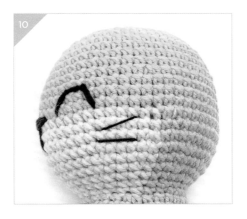

ACCESSORIES

Fish

Fish and Leaf

Rounds 1-2: Using Light Yellow, repeat Rounds 1-2 of Arm.
At the end of Round 2, there are 8 sc.
Round 3: [Sc in each of next 3 sts, inc in next st] 2 times. (10 sc)
Round 4: [Sc in each of next 4 sts, inc in next st] 2 times. (12 sc)
Round 5: [Sc in each of next 5 sts, inc in next st] 2 times, change to Orange. (14 sc) Fasten off Light Yellow.
Alternate Orange and Yellow every two rounds.
Rounds 6-12: *(7 Rounds)* Sc in each st around. (14 sc)
Round 13: [Sc in each of next 5 sts, sc-dec] 2 times. (12 sc)

» Start stuffing Fish, adding more as you go.

Round 14: Sc in each st around. (12 sc)
Round 15: [Sc in each of next 2 sts, sc-dec] 3 times. (9 sc)
Round 16: Sc in each st around. (9 sc)
Round 17: [Sc in next st, sc-dec] 3 times. (6 sc)

» Do not stuff from here.

Round 18: [2 sc in next st] 6 times. (12 sc)
Round 19: Sc in each st around. (12 sc) Fasten off Yellow.
Last Row: Flatten the last round and working through both thicknesses, with Orange, sc in each of next 6 sc. Fasten off, leaving a long tail for sewing.

Leaf

Using Kiwi, ch 6, starting in the second ch from hook, sc in next ch, hdc in next ch, dc in next ch, hdc in next ch, (sc, ch 3, sc) in the last ch; working in unused loops on other side of starting ch, hdc in next ch, dc in next ch, hdc in next ch, sc in next ch; join with sl st to first sc; ch 2. Fasten off, leaving a long tail for sewing.

Fish

» Using long tail, insert needle and bring out at center of Fish (image 24). Position and sew the Fish onto Body (images 25 & 26).

Leaf

» With wrong side of Leaf facing, using long tail, insert needle and bring out at center of Leaf (image 27). With right side facing (image 28), position and sew the Leaf on Head, at Round 6, between the Ears (image 29).

Face

» Using a small makeup brush, apply blusher to the cheeks (image 30).

Lily The Lamb

When you're walking through the meadow, and spot something blue, look carefully! It's probably Lily wearing her beautiful new outfit. What a lovely dress! It's easy to recognize this sweet, little lamb - she's the prettiest in the flock!

MATERIALS

Scheepjes Softfun Denim

Color A: Light Blue (509)

Scheepjes Catona

Main Color (MC): Snow White (106)
Color B: Sky Blue (510)
Color C: Baby Blue (509)
Old Rose (408) & Powder Pink (238) - small amounts for Flower

Sizes B-1 (2.25 mm) (Main Hook) & C-2 (2.75 mm) Crochet Hooks - or sizes suitable for yarn used. (Use Main Hook throughout, unless otherwise stated.)
Yarn Needle
Stitch Markers
⁵⁄₁₆"(8 mm) Safety Eyes - 2
Small Beads or Buttons - 2
Thread and needle - for sewing on Beads / Buttons
Toy Stuffing
Cosmetic Blusher & Brush - for Cheeks

Finished Size
About 8¾" (22 cm) tall

Skill Level
♥ ♥

SPECIAL STITCH

Bobble Stitch (bob): Yarn over, insert hook in stitch or space specified and pull up a loop (3 loops on hook), yarn over and draw through 2 loops on hook (2 loops remain on hook) (image a); [yarn over, insert hook in same stitch or space and pull up a loop, yarn over and draw through 2 loops on hook] 3 times (5 loops remain on hook) (image b), yarn over and draw through all 5 loops on hook (image c).

HEAD

Round 1: Using MC, make a Magic Ring; ch 1, 8 sc in ring, DO NOT JOIN. (8 sc) Tug tail to tighten ring. Mark last stitch.

Round 2: Inc in each st around. (16 sc) Move marker each round.

Round 3: [Sc in next st, inc in next st] 8 times. (24 sc)

Round 4: [Sc in each of next 2 sts, inc in next st] 8 times. (32 sc)

Round 5: [Sc in each of next 3 sts, inc in next st] 8 times. (40 sc)

Round 6: Sc in each st around. (40 sc)

Round 7: [Sc in each of next 4 sts, inc in next st] 8 times. (48 sc)

Rounds 8-11: *(4 Rounds)* Sc in each st around. (48 sc)

Round 12: [Sc in each of next 7 sts, inc in next st] 6 times. (54 sc)

Rounds 13-15: *(3 Rounds)* Sc in each st around. (54 sc)

Round 16: [Sc in each of next 8 sts, inc in next st] 6 times. (60 sc)

Round 17: [Sc in each of next 8 sts, **sc-dec**] 6 times. (54 sc)

Round 18: Sc in each of next 3 sts, sc-dec, [sc in each of next 7 sts, sc-dec] 5 times, sc in each of next 4 sts. (48 sc)

Round 19: [Sc in each of next 6 sts, sc-dec] 6 times. (42 sc)

Round 20: Sc in each of next 2 sts, sc-dec, [sc in each of next 5 sts, sc-dec] 5 times, sc in each of next 3 sts. (36 sc)

Round 21 [Sc in each of next 4 sts, sc-dec] 6 times. (30 sc)

» Insert Safety Eyes between Rounds 13 & 14, about 9 stitches apart.

» Start stuffing Head, adding more as you go.

Round 22: Sc in next st, sc-dec, [sc in each of next 3 sts, sc-dec] 5 times, sc in each of next 2 sts. (24 sc)

Round 23: [Sc in each of next 4 sts, sc-dec] 4 times. (20 sc) Sl st in next st. Fasten off, leaving a long tail for sewing.

HAT

Round 1: Using Color A and larger hook, make a Magic Ring; ch 1, 6 sc in ring; join with a sl st to first sc. (6 sc) Tug tail to tighten ring.

Round 2: Ch 2, (**bob**, hdc) in each st around; join with sl st to first bobble. (6 bobble sts & 6 hdc) Join all bobble-rounds in this manner.

Round 3: Ch 1, inc in each st around; join with sl st to first sc. (24 sc) Join all sc-rounds in this manner.

Round 4: Ch 2, [bob in next st, hdc in next st] 12 times; join. (12 bobble sts & 12 hdc)

Round 5: Ch 1, [sc in each of next 3 sts, inc in next st] 6 times; join. (30 sc)

Round 6: Ch 2, [bob in next st, hdc in next st] 15 times; join. (15 bobble sts & 15 hdc)

Round 7: Ch 1, [sc in each of next 4 sts, inc in next st] 6 times; join. (36 sc)

Round 8: Ch 2, [bob in next st, hdc in next st] 18 times; join. (18 bobble sts & 18 hdc)

Round 9: Ch 1, sc in each st around; join. (36 sc)

Round 10: Ch 2, hdc in each st around; join with sl st to first hdc. (36 hdc)

Round 11: *(Ruffle)* Working in FLO, [ch 3, sl st in next st] 36 times. Fasten off, leaving a long tail for sewing (image 1).

BODY

Rounds 1-5: Using MC, repeat Rounds 1-5 of Head. At the end of Round 5, there are 40 sc.

Rounds 6-9: *(4 Rounds)* Sc in each st around. (40 sc)

Round 10: [Sc in each of next 6 sts, sc-dec] 5 times. (35 sc)

Rounds 11-12: *(2 Rounds)* Sc in each st around. (35 sc)

Round 13: [Sc in each of next 5 sts, sc-dec] 5 times. (30 sc)

Rounds 14-15: *(2 Rounds)* Sc in each st around. (30 sc)

Round 16: [Sc in each of next 4 sts, sc-dec] 5 times. (25 sc)

Rounds 17-18: *(2 Rounds)* Sc in each st around. (25 sc)

Round 19: Working in BLO, [sc in each of next 3 sts, sc-dec] 5 times. (20 sc)

» Stuff Body firmly.

Fasten off, leaving a long tail for sewing.

EAR (Make 2)

Round 1: Using MC, make a Magic Ring; ch 1, 8 sc in ring, DO NOT JOIN. (8 sc) Tug tail to tighten ring. Mark last stitch.

Round 2: [Inc in next st, sc in next st] 4 times. (12 sc) Move marker each round.

Round 3: Sc in each st around. (12 sc)

Round 4: [Sc in each of next 2 sts, inc in next st] 4 times. (16 sc)

Round 5: Sc in each st around. (16 sc)

Round 6: [Sc in each of next 3 sts, inc in next st] 4 times. (20 sc)

Rounds 7-9: *(3 Rounds)* Sc in each st around. (20 sc)

Round 10: [Sc in each of next 3 sts, sc-dec] 4 times. (16 sc)

Round 11: Sc in each st around. (16 sc)

Round 12: [Sc in each of next 2 sts, sc-dec] 4 times. (12 sc)

Last Row: Flatten the last round and working through both thicknesses, sc in each of next 6 sc. Fasten off, leaving a long tail for sewing.

Note: *Arms are not stuffed.*

Round 1: Using MC, make a Magic Ring; ch 1, 7 sc in ring, DO NOT JOIN. (7 sc) Tug tail to tighten ring. Mark last stitch, move the marker each round.

Rounds 2-14: *(13 Rounds)* Sc in each st around. (7 sc)

Last Row: Flatten the last round and working through both thicknesses, sc in each of next 3 sc. Fasten off, leaving a long tail for sewing.

LEG (Make 2)

Rounds 1-2: Using Color B, repeat Rounds 1-2 of Head. At the end of Round 2, there are 16 sc.

Round 3: Sc in next st, inc in next st, sc in each of next 4 sts, inc in each of next 4 sts, sc in each of next 4 sts, inc in next st, sc in last st. (22 sc)

Rounds 4-6: *(3 Rounds)* Sc in each st around. (22 sc)

Round 7: Sc in each of next 7 sts, [sc-dec] 4 times, sc in each of next 7 sts. (18 sc)

Round 8: Sc in each st around. (18 sc)

Round 9: Sc in each of next 5 sts, [sc-dec] 4 times, sc in each of next 5 sts. (14 sc)

Round 10: Sc in each of next 6 sts, sc-dec, sc in each of next 6 sts. (13 sc)

Rounds 11-14: *(4 Rounds)* Sc in each st around. (13 sc) At the end of the Round 14, change to MC. Fasten off Color B.

» Start stuffing Leg firmly, adding more as you go.

Round 15: Working in BLO, [sc in next st, sc-dec] 4 times, sc in last st. (9 sc)

Note: *I prefer to work the Shoe Detail at this point, before continuing with the Leg.*

Rounds 16-28: *(13 Rounds)* Sc in each st around. (9 sc)

Round 29: Sc in each st around, ending at center back of Leg, adding additional sc-sts if needed.

Last Row: Flatten the last round and working through both thicknesses, sc in each of next 4 sc. Fasten off, leaving a long tail for sewing.

Shoe Detail

Working in the FLO of Round 14, attach Color C to first st (image 2), [ch 2, sl st in next st] 13 times. Fasten off, leaving a long tail for embroidery.

» Using long tail, embroider small lines across front of Shoe (images 3, 4 & 5). Weave in ends.

» Position the completed Legs on either side at Round 7 of the Body. Using long tails and yarn needle, sew them in place (image 6).

DRESS

Round 1: With Legs facing upwards, working in FLO of Round 18 of Body, using larger hook, attach Color A to last st (image 7), ch 1, sc in each st around (image 8); join with sl st to first sc. (25 sc) Join all sc-rounds in this manner.

Round 2: Working in BLO, ch 2, dc in each st around; join with sl st to first dc. (25 dc) Join all dc-rounds in this manner.

Round 3: Ch 1, [sc in each of next 4 st, inc in next st] 5 times; join. (30 sc)

Round 4: Ch 2, dc in each st around; join. (30 dc)

Round 5: Ch 1, sc in each st around; join. (30 sc)

Round 6: Ch 2, dc in each st around; join. (30 dc)

Round 7: Ch 1, [sc in each of next 4 st, inc in next st] 6 times; join. (36 sc)

Round 8: Ch 2, dc in each st around; join. (36 dc)

Round 9: Ch 1, sc in each st around; join. (36 sc)

Round 10: Ch 2, [hdc in next st, bob in next st, hdc in next st] 12 times; join with sl st to first hdc. (24 hdc & 12 bobble sts)

Round 11: Ch 1, sc in each st around; join. (36 sc)

Round 12: Ch 2, [bob in next st, hdc in each of next 2 sts] 12 times; join with sl st to first bobble. (24 hdc & 12 bobble sts)

Round 13: Ch 1, sc in each st around; join. (36 sc)

Round 14: Ch 2, [hdc in each of next 2 sts, bob in next st] 12 times; fasten off with invisible join. (24 hdc & 12 bobble sts)

COLLAR

Row 1: With Legs facing upwards, working in FLO of Round 1 of Dress, attach Color B to st at center front (image 10), ch 1, sc in first st, hdc in next st, dc in each of next 21 st, hdc in next st, sc in last st. (25 sts)

Row 2: Ch 1, turn, sc in first st, hdc in next st, dc in each of next 2 sts, [2 dc in next st, dc in each of next 3 sts] 4 times, 2 dc in next st, dc in each of next 2 sts, hdc in next st, sc in last st, change to Color C. (30 sts)

Row 3: *(Ruffle)* Turn, [ch 4, sl st in next st] 30 times. Fasten off and weave in ends (image 11).

FLOWER

Using Old Rose, ch 27, starting in the third ch from hook, [3 dc in next ch, sc in next ch] 5 times; change to Powder Pink, [3 dc in each of next 2 ch, sc in next ch] 5 times. Fasten off, leaving a long tail for sewing.

» Roll the Flower into shape, and using tail, sew to secure. (images 12-13)

ASSEMBLY (use photos as guide)

Nose - Using Old Rose and yarn needle, embroider a Nose between the Eyes (image 14).

Hat - Position the Hat on Head and sew in place (image 15).

Ears - Using long tail and yarn needle, fold the last round of Ear in half, and sew edges together (image 16). Repeat for other ear. Position Ears on Head at Round 7 of Hat and sew in place (images 17 & 18).

Flower - Position and sew the Flower on Hat (image 19).

Arms - Position the Arms on either side of the Body, about Round 3 of Dress. Using long tails and yarn needle, sew them in place, working through the Dress into the Body, to secure them (image 20).

Beads - Sew the Beads to the front of Dress (image 21).

Head - Sew the Head to Body.

Face - Using a small makeup brush, apply blusher to the cheeks and the inside of Ears.

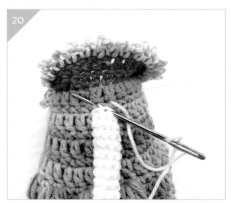

Nana

Fall (Autumn) is Nana's favorite season of the year. Her wardrobe is full of warm clothing, like hats and scarves. She loves being in the forest, taking photos of her friends, against the backdrop of the changing colors of the leaves.

MATERIALS

Scheepjes Catona

Main Color (MC): Bridal White (105)
Color A: Root Beer (157)
Color B: Topaz (179)

Scheepjes Merino Soft

Color C: Gauguin (619)

Scheepjes Softfun

Mustard (2621) - for Hair
Red (2410) - for Hat & Scarf

Scheepjes Maxi Sweet Treat (Cotton Thread)

Black Coffee (162) - for Eyes & Bow

Sizes B-1 (2.25 mm) (Main Hook) & C-2 (2.75 mm) Crochet Hooks - or sizes suitable for yarn used. (Use Main Hook throughout, unless otherwise stated.)
Yarn Needle
Embroidery Needle
Stitch Markers
Small Button - for Hat
Button - for Scarf
Thread and needle - for sewing on buttons
Small piece of fabric ⅜" (1 cm) wide by 2" (5 cm) long - for Bow
Toy Stuffing
Cosmetic Blusher & Brush - for Cheeks

Finished Size
About 8½" (22 cm) tall

Skill Level
 ♥ ♥

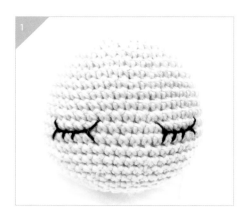

HEAD

Round 1: Using MC, make a Magic Ring; ch 1, 8 sc in ring, DO NOT JOIN. (8 sc) Tug tail to tighten ring. Mark last stitch.

Round 2: Inc in each st around. (16 sc) Move marker each round.

Round 3: [Sc in next st, inc in next st] 8 times. (24 sc)

Round 4: [Sc in each of next 2 sts, inc in next st] 8 times. (32 sc)

Round 5: [Sc in each of next 3 sts, inc in next st] 8 times. (40 sc)

Round 6: Sc in each st around. (40 sc)

Round 7: [Sc in each of next 4 sts, inc in next st] 8 times. (48 sc)

Rounds 8-11: *(4 Rounds)* Sc in each st around. (48 sc)

Round 12: [Sc in each of next 7 sts, inc in next st] 6 times. (54 sc)

Rounds 13-15: *(3 Rounds)* Sc in each st around. (54 sc)

Round 16: [Sc in each of next 8 sts, inc in next st] 6 times. (60 sc)

Round 17: [Sc in each of next 8 sts, **sc-dec**] 6 times. (54 sc)

Round 18: Sc in each of next 3 sts, sc-dec, [sc in each of next 7 sts, sc-dec] 5 times, sc in each of next 4 sts. (48 sc)

Round 19: [Sc in each of next 6 sts, sc-dec] 6 times. (42 sc)

Round 20: Sc in each of next 2 sts, sc-dec, [sc in each of next 5 sts, sc-dec] 5 times, sc in each of next 3 sts. (36 sc)

Round 21: [Sc in each of next 4 sts, sc-dec] 6 times. (30 sc)

» Start stuffing Head, adding more as you go.

Round 22: Sc in next st, sc-dec, [sc in each of next 3 sts, sc-dec] 5 times, sc in each of next 2 sts. (24 sc)

Round 23: [Sc in each of next 4 sts, sc-dec] 4 times. (20 sc). Sl st in next st. Fasten off, leaving a long tail for sewing.

» Using Cotton Thread, embroider the sleeping eyes (over 5 sts) between Rounds 13 & 14, with 5 sts between each eye (image 1).

ARM (Make 2)

Note: *Arms are not stuffed.*

Round 1: Using MC, make a Magic Ring; ch 1, 6 sc in ring, DO NOT JOIN. (6 sc) Tug tail to tighten ring. Mark last stitch.

Round 2: [Inc in next st, sc in next st] 3 times. (9 sc) Move marker each round.

Rounds 3-4: *(2 Rounds)* Sc in each of next st around. (9 sc)

Round 5: [Sc-dec, sc in next st] 3 times, change to Color C. (6 sc) Fasten off MC.

Round 6: Working in BLO, inc in each st around. (12 sc)

Round 7: Inc in each st around. (24 sc)

Round 8: Sc in each st around. (24 sc)

Round 9: [Sc in each of next 4 sts, sc-dec] 4 times. (20 sc)

Round 10: [Sc in each of next 2 sts, sc-dec] 5 times. (15 sc)

Round 11: [Sc in next st, sc-dec] 5 times, change to Color A. (10 sc)

Round 12: Sc in each st around, change to Color C. (10 sc)

Rounds 13-14: *(2 Rounds)* Sc in each st around. (10 sc) At the end of Round 14, change to Color A.

Round 15: Sc in each st around, change to Color C. (10 sc) Fasten off Color A.

Rounds 16-20: *(5 Rounds)* Sc in each st around. (10 sc)

Last Row: Flatten the last round and working through both thicknesses, sc in each of next 5 sc. Fasten off and leave a tail for sewing.

Sleeve Detail

Working in FLO of Round 5, attach Color B (image 2) to any st, [ch 2, sl st in next st] 6 times. Fasten off and weave in ends (image 3).

BODY

Rounds 1-5: Using Color B, repeat Rounds 1-5 of Head. At the end of Round 5, there are 40 sc.

Rounds 6-9: *(4 Rounds)* Sc in each st around. (40 sc)

Round 10: [Sc in each of next 6 sts, sc-dec] 5 times. (35 sc)

Rounds 11-12: *(2 Rounds)* Sc in each st around. (35 sc)

Round 13: [Sc in each of next 5 sts, sc-dec] 5 times. (30 sc)

Rounds 14-15: *(2 Rounds)* Sc in each st around. (30 sc)

Round 16: [Sc in each of next 4 sts, sc-dec] 5 times. (25 sc)

Rounds 17-18: *(2 Rounds)* Sc in each st around. (25 sc)

Round 19: Working in BLO, [sc in each of next 3 sts, sc-dec] 5 times. (20 sc)

» Stuff Body firmly.

Fasten off, leaving a long tail for sewing.

LEG (Make 2)

Rounds 1-2: Using Color A, repeat Rounds 1-2 of Head. At the end of Round 2, there are 16 sc.

Round 3: Sc in next st, inc in next st, sc in each of next 4 sts, inc in each of next 4 sts, sc in each of next 4 sts, inc in next st, sc in last st. (22 sc)

Rounds 4-6: *(3 Rounds)* Sc in each st around. (22 sc)

Round 7: Sc in each of next 7 sts, [sc-dec] 4 times, sc in each of next 7 sts. (18 sc)

Round 8: Sc in each st around. (18 sc)

Round 9: Sc in each of next 5 sts, [sc-dec] 4 times, sc in each of next 5 sts. (14 sc)

Round 10: Sc in each of next 6 sts, sc-dec, sc in each of next 6 sts. (13 sc)

Rounds 11-14: *(4 Rounds)* Sc in each st around. (13 sc) At the end of the Round 14, change to MC. Fasten off Color A.

» Start stuffing Leg firmly, adding more as you go.

Round 15: Working in BLO, [sc in next st, sc-dec] 4 times, sc in last st. (9 sc)

Rounds 16-30: *(15 Rounds)* Sc in each st around. (9 sc)

Round 31: Sc in each st around, ending at center back of Leg, adding additional sc-sts if needed.

Last Row: Flatten the last round and working through both thicknesses, sc in each of next 4 sc. Fasten off, leaving a long tail for sewing.

Shoe Detail

Working in the FLO of Round 14, attach Color B to the last st (image 4), [ch 2, sl st in next st] 13 times. Fasten off, leaving a long tail for embroidery.

» Using long tail, embroider small lines across front of Shoe (images 5 & 6). Weave in ends (image 7).

» Position the completed Legs on either side at Round 7 of the Body. Using long tails and yarn needle, sew them in place (image 8).

DRESS

Round 1: With Legs facing upwards, working in FLO of Round 18 of Body, using larger hook, attach Color C to last st (image 9), ch 2, dc in each st around; join with sl st to first dc. (25 dc) Join all dc-rounds in this manner.

Round 2: Ch 2, [dc in each of next 4 sts, 2 dc in next st] 5 times; join. (30 dc)

Round 3: Ch 2, dc in each st; join. (30 dc)

Round 4: Ch 2, [dc in each of next 5 sts, 2 dc in next st] 5 times; join. (35 dc)

Round 5: Ch 2, dc in each st around; join. (35 dc)

Round 6: Ch 2, [dc in each of next 6 sts, 2 dc in next st] 5 times; join. (40 dc)

Round 7: Ch 2, dc in each st around; join; change to Color A. (40 dc)

Round 8: Ch 1, [sc in each of next 9 sts, inc in next st] 4 times; join with sl st to first sc; change to Color C. (44 sc)

Round 9: Ch 2, hdc in each st around; join with sl st to first hdc; change to Color A. (44 hdc)

Round 10: Ch 1, sc in each st around; join with sl st to first sc; change to Color C. (44 sc) Fasten off Color A.

Round 11: Ch 2, hdc in each st around; join with sl st to first hdc; change to Color B. (44 hdc) Fasten off Color C.

Round 12: Working in BLO, ch 2, [hdc in next st, 3 hdc in next st] 22 times; fasten off with invisible join. (88 sts)

HAIR

Rounds 1-11: Using Mustard and larger hook, repeat Rounds 1-11 of Head. At the end of Round 11, there are 48 sts.

Round 12: *(Hair strands)* *Sl st in next st; ch 7, starting in second ch from hook, [2 sc in next st, sc in next st] 3 times (9 sc); sl st in next st; repeat from * 23 times more. (24 strands) Fasten off, leaving a very long tail for sewing (image 10).

SCARF

Row 1: (Right Side) Using Red and larger hook, ch 7, starting in third ch from hook, dc in each ch across. (5 dc)

Rows 2-33: *(32 Rows)* Ch 2, turn, dc in each st across. (5 dc) At the end of Row 33, fasten off, leaving a long tail for sewing.

HAT

Rounds 1-5: Using Red and larger hook, repeat Rounds 1-5 of Head. At the end of Round 5, there are 40 sts.

Round 6: [Sc in each of next 4 sts, inc in next st] 8 times. (48 sc)

Round 7: [Sc in each of next 5 sts, inc in next st] 8 times. (56 sc)

Round 8: [Sc in each of next 6 sts, inc in next st] 8 times. (64 sc)

Round 9: [Sc in each of next 7 sts, inc in next st] 8 times. (72 sc)

Round 10: [Sc in each of next 8 sts, inc in next st] 8 times. (80 sc)

Round 11: [Sc in each of next 8 sts, sc-dec] 8 times. (72 sc)

Round 12: [Sc in each of next 7 sts, sc-dec] 8 times. (64 sc)

Round 13: [Sc in each of next 6 sts, sc-dec] 8 times. (56 sc)

Round 14: [Sc in each of next 5 sts, sc-dec] 8 times. (48 sc)

Round 15: [Sc in each of next 4 sts, sc-dec] 8 times. (40 sc)

Round 16: Ch 1, hdc in each st around; join with sl st to first hdc. (40 hdc) Fasten off and weave in ends.

» Sew ends of fabric strip together to create a ring. Flatten the ring (with seam in center) and wind Cotton Thread tightly around center, to create a bow. Sew Bow to side of Hat (image 11).

» Sew Small Button to crown of Hat (image 12).

ASSEMBLY (use photos as guide)

Arms - Position the Arms on either side of the Body (at Round 2 of Dress). Using long tails and yarn needle, sew them in place, working through the Dress into the Body, to secure them (image 13).

Hair - Place Hair on Head, using pins to keep it in place (images 14 & 15). Using long tail, sew the strands in place.

Head - Sew the Head to Body.

Face - Using a small makeup brush, apply blusher to the cheeks.

Scarf - Wrap Scarf around neck and position Button with a pin (image 16). Sew Button in place.

Hat - Position Hat on Head.

Pio The Hippo

Pio is a very shy young hippopotamus. He doesn't talk much, but boy, he sure is a good listener. When you see him, be sure to give him a hug!

MATERIALS

Scheepjes Softfun

Main Color (MC): Light Grey (2530)
Color A: Cream (2426)
Color B: Sienna (2431)
Color C: Light Pink (2513)

Scheepjes Maxi Sweet Treat (Cotton Thread)

Black Coffee (162) - for Eyebrows

Size C-2 (2.75 mm) Crochet Hook - or size suitable for yarn used.
Yarn Needle
Embroidery Needle
Stitch Markers
5⁄16″ (8 mm) Safety Eyes - 2
Toy Stuffing
Cosmetic Blusher & Brush - for Cheeks

Finished Size
About 7 ⅞″ (20 cm) tall

Skill Level
♥

HEAD & BODY

Round 1: Starting at Head, using MC, make a Magic Ring; ch 1, 8 sc in ring, DO NOT JOIN. (8 sc) Tug tail to tighten ring. Mark last stitch.

Round 2: Inc in each st around. (16 sc) Move marker each round.

Round 3 [Sc in next st, inc in next st] 8 times. (24 sc)

Round 4: [Sc in each of next 2 sts, inc in next st] 8 times. (32 sc)

Round 5: [Sc in each of next 3 sts, inc in next st] 8 times. (40 sc)

Round 6: Sc in next st, inc in next st, [sc in each of next 4 sts, inc in next st] 7 times, sc in each of next 3 sts. (48 sc)

Round 7: [Sc in each of next 7 sts, inc in next st] 6 times. (54 sc)

Rounds 8-17: *(10 Rounds)* Sc in each st around. (54 sc)

» Mark the 16th st of Round 17 with a piece of yarn. This is the center point between the Eyes (image 1).

Round 18: Sc in each of next 8 sts, [inc in next st, sc in each of next 2 sts] 6 times, sc in each of next 28 sts. (60 sc)

Round 19: [Inc in next st, sc in each of next 3 sts] 10 times, sc in each of next 20 sts. (70 sc)

Rounds 20-24: *(5 Rounds)* Sc in each st around. (70 sc)

Round 25: [**Sc-dec**, sc in each of next 3 sts] 10 times, sc in each of next 20 sts. (60 sc)

Rounds 26-28: *(3 Rounds)* Sc in each st around. (60 sc)

Round 29: Sc in each of next 8 sts, [sc-dec, sc in each of next 2 sts] 6 times, sc in each of next 28 sts (54 sc)

Round 30: [Sc-dec, sc in each of next 7 sts] 6 times. (48 sc)

Round 31: [Sc in each of next 4 sts, sc-dec] 8 times. (40 sc)

Round 32: [Sc in each of next 3 sts, sc-dec] 8 times. (32 sc)

Round 33: [Sc in each of next 2 sts, sc-dec] 8 times, change to Color A. (24 sc) Fasten off MC.

» Insert Safety Eyes between Rounds 16 & 17, about 8 stitches apart (using marked center point).

» Stuff Head firmly, but not the Neck part.

Alternate Color A and Color B every three rounds.

Round 34: [Sc in each of next 2 sts, inc in next st] 8 times. (32 sc)

Round 35: [Sc in each of next 3 sts, inc in next st] 8 times. (40 sc)

Rounds 36-39: *(4 Rounds)* Sc in each st around. (40 sc)

Round 40: [Sc in each of next 4 sts, inc in next st] 8 times. (48 sc)

Rounds 41-46: *(6 Rounds)* Sc in each st around. (48 sc)

Round 47: [Sc in each of next 5 sts, inc in next st] 8 times. (56 sc)

Rounds 48-50: *(3 Rounds)* Sc in each st around. (56 sc) At the end of Round 50, change to MC. Leave Color B hanging on the outside (image 2). Fasten off Color A.

» Start stuffing Neck & Body firmly, adding more as you go.

Round 51: Working in BLO, sc in each st around. (56 sc)

Rounds 52-55: *(4 Rounds)* Sc in each st around. (56 sc)

Round 56: [Sc-dec, sc in each of next 5 sts] 8 times. (48 sc)

Round 57: Sc in each st around. (48 sc)

Round 58: [Sc-dec, sc in each of next 4 sts] 8 times. (40 sc)

Round 59: [Sc-dec, sc in each of next 3 sts] 8 times. (32 sc)

Round 60: [Sc-dec, sc in each of next 2 sts] 8 times. (24 sc)

Round 61: [Sc-dec, sc in next sts] 8 times. (16 sc)

Round 62: [Sc-dec] 8 times. (8 sc)

» Finish stuffing the Body.

Fasten off and close remaining sts, weaving in end.

Sweater Detail

With Head pointing down, working in FLO of Round 50, insert hook in first st and pick up Color B (image 3), ch 1, sc in each st around; fasten off with invisible join. (56 sc).

ARM (Make 2)

Rounds 1-3: Using Color C, repeat Rounds 1-3 of Head. At the end of Round 3, change to MC in last st. (24 sc) Fasten off Color C.

Rounds 4-9: *(6 Rounds)* Sc in each st around. (24)

Round 10: [Sc in each of next 4 sts, sc-dec] 4 times. (20 sc)

Rounds 11-13: *(3 Rounds)* Sc in each st around. (20 sc) At the end of Round 13, change to Color B. Fasten off MC.

Round 14: Sc in each st around. (20 sc)

Round 15: Working in BLO, sc in each st around. (20 sc)

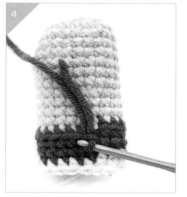  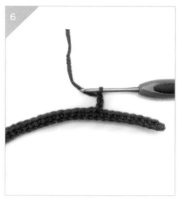 

Round 16: Sc in each st around, change to Color A. (20 sc) Fasten off Color B.

Round 17: [Sc in each of next 3 sts, sc-dec] 4 times. (16 sc)

Note: *I prefer to work the Arm Detail at this point, before continuing with the Arm.*

Rounds 18-19: *(2 Rounds)* Sc in each st around. (16 sc)

» Stuff Arm.

Last Row: Flatten the last round and working through both thicknesses, sc in each of next 8 sc. Fasten off, leaving a long tail for sewing.

Arm Detail: With hand facing upwards, working in the FLO of Round 14, attach Color B to the last st (image 4), ch 1, sc in each st around; fasten off with invisible join. (20 sc) (image 5).

LEG (Make 2)

Rounds 1-3: Using Color C, repeat Rounds 1-3 of Head. At the end of Round 3, change to MC in last st. (24 sc) Fasten off Color C.

Round 4: [Sc in each of next 2 sts, inc in next st] 8 times. (32 sc)

Rounds 5-7: *(3 Rounds)* Sc in each st around. (32)

Round 8: [Sc in each of next 6 sts, sc-dec] 4 times. (28 sc)

Round 9: Sc in each st around. (28 sc)

Round 10: [Sc in each of next 5 sts, sc-dec] 4 times. (24 sc)

Rounds 11-14: *(4 Rounds)* Sc in each st around. (24 sc)

Round 15: [Sc in each of next 4 sts, sc-dec] 4 times. (20 sc)

Round 16: Sc in each st around. (20 sc)

Round 17: [Sc in each of next 3 sts, sc-dec] 4 times. (16 sc)

» Stuff Leg.

Last Row: Flatten the last round and working through both thicknesses, sc in each of next 8 sc. Fasten off, leaving a long tail for sewing.

EAR (Make 2)

Round 1: Using MC, make a Magic Ring; ch 1, 6 sc in ring, DO NOT JOIN. (6 sc) Tug tail to tighten ring. Mark last stitch.

Round 2: Inc in each st around. (12 sc) Move marker each round.

Rounds 3-4: *(2 Rounds)* Sc in each st around. (12 sc)

Round 5: [Sc-dec, sc in each of next 2 sts] 3 times. (9 sc) Sl st in next st. Fasten off, leaving a long tail for sewing.

NOSTRIL (Make 2)

Using Color C, make a Magic Ring; ch 1, 4 sc in ring, DO NOT JOIN. (4 sc) Tug tail to tighten ring. Fasten off, leaving a long tail for sewing.

TAIL

Round 1: Using MC, make a Magic Ring; ch 1, 6 sc in ring, DO NOT JOIN. (6 sc) Tug tail to tighten ring. Mark last stitch.

Round 2: [Inc in next st, sc in next st] 3 times. (9 sc) Move marker each round.

Round 3: Sc in each st around. (9 sc)

Round 4: [Sc in each of next 2 sts, inc in next st] 3 times. (12 sc)

Round 5: Sc in each st around. (12 sc)

Round 6: [Sc in each of next 5 sts, inc in next st] 2 times. (14 sc)

Round 7: Sc in each st around. (14 sc) Sl st in next st. Fasten off, leaving a long tail for sewing.

COLLAR

Row 1: (Right Side) Using Color B, ch 65, starting in the second ch from hook, sc in each ch across. (64 sc) Fasten off and weave in ends.

Row 2: With right side facing, attach Color B to the 10th st (image 6), ch 3, dc in each of next 38 sts. (38 dc) Leave remaining 16 sts unworked.

Row 3: Ch 1, turn, sc in each st across. (38 sc) Fasten off and weave in ends (image 7).

ASSEMBLY (use photos as guide)

Ears - Position Ears at Round 8 on either side of Head, 25 sts apart, and sew in place (image 8).

Nostrils - Sew Nostrils 3 rounds below each Eye, about 12 sts apart (image 9).

Eyebrows - Using Cotton Thread, embroider a straight stitch, two rounds above each Eye.

Arms - Position Arms on either side of the Body (2 rounds below Neck). Using long tails and yarn needle, sew them in place (image 10).

Legs - Position Legs on either side of the Body (below Sweater Detail). Using long tails and yarn needle, sew them in place (images 11 & 12).

Tail - Position the Tail to center back of Body, 2 rounds below Sweater Detail. Sew in place, stuffing before closing (image 13).

Collar - Wrap the Collar around neck, and tie in front.

Face - Using a small makeup brush, apply blusher to the cheeks and the inside of Ears.

Rosie Horse

Rosie is a day-dreamer, with her head in the clouds. When it's raining outside, she dresses up in her elegant pink outfit, makes a pot of tea, and then sits and listens to the rhythm of the rain drops, making up songs in her head.

MATERIALS

Scheepjes Softfun

Main Color (MC): White (2412)
Color A: Cream (2426)
Color B: Light Pink (2513)
Color C: Rose Pink (2608)

Scheepjes Catona

Lemon Chiffon (100), Lime Juice (392), Baby Blue (509), Bluebell (173) - small amounts for Flowers

Scheepjes Maxi Sweet Treat (Cotton Thread)

Black (110) - for sleeping Eyes

Size C-2 (2.75 mm) Crochet Hook - or size suitable for yarn used.
Yarn Needle
Embroidery Needle
Stitch Markers
Toy Stuffing
Cosmetic Blusher & Brush
- for Cheeks & Ears

Finished Size
About 13½" (35 cm) tall, when standing;
about 9½" (24 cm) when sitting

Skill Level

SPECIAL STITCH

Pattern Stitch: (for Body) [Insert hook in next st, pull up loop in Color B (image 1), using MC, yarn over and draw through both loops on hook (image 2), sc in each of next 2 sts] around.

Note: *Use Stranding Method for Color B.*

HEAD

Round 1: Starting at Snout, using Color A, make a Magic Ring; ch 1, 6 sc in ring, DO NOT JOIN. (6 sc) Tug tail to tighten ring. Mark last stitch.

Round 2: Inc in each st around. (12 sc) Move marker each round.

Round 3: [Sc in next st, inc in next st] 6 times. (18 sc)

Round 4: [Sc in each of next 2 sts, inc in next st] 6 times. (24 sc)

Round 5: Sc in next st, inc in next st, [sc in each of next 3 sts, inc in next st] 5 times, sc in each of next 2 sts. (30 sc)

Round 6: [Sc in each of next 4 sts, inc in next st] 6 times. (36 sc)

Round 7: [Sc in each of next 5 sts, inc in next st] 6 times. (42 sc)

Rounds 8-10: *(3 Rounds)* Sc in each st around. (42 sc) At the end of Round 10, change to MC. Fasten off Color A.

Rounds 11-14: *(4 Rounds)* Sc in each st around. (42 sc)

Round 15: Sc in each of next 16 sts, [inc in next st, sc in next st] 6 times, sc in each of next 14 sts. (48 sc)

Rounds 16-18: *(3 Rounds)* Sc in each st around. (48 sc)

Round 19: Sc in each of next 14 sts, [inc in next st, sc in each of next 2 sts] 8 times, sc in each of next 10 sts. (56 sc)

Rounds 20-29: *(10 Rounds)* Sc in each st around. (56 sc)

Round 30: [Sc in each of next 6 sts, **sc-dec**] 7 times. (49 sc)

Rounds 31-32: *(2 Rounds)* Sc in each st around. (49 sc)

Round 33: [Sc in each of next 5 sts, sc-dec] 7 times. (42 sc)

» Start stuffing Head, adding more as you go.

Rounds 34-35: *(2 Rounds)* Sc in each st around. (42 sc)

Round 36: [Sc in each of next 4 sts, sc-dec] 7 times. (35 sc)

Round 37: [Sc in each of next 3 sts, sc-dec] 7 times. (28 sc)

Round 38: [Sc in each of next 2 sts, sc-dec] 7 times. (21 sc)

Round 39: [Sc in each of next st, sc-dec] 7 times. (14 sc)

Round 40: [Sc-dec] 7 times. (7 sc)

» Finish stuffing Head.

Fasten off and close remaining sts, weaving in end.

BODY

Rounds 1-7: Starting at base, using MC, repeat Rounds 1-7 of Head. At the end of Round 7, there are 42 sc.

Round 8: Sc in each of next 3 sts, inc in next st, [sc in each of next 6 sts, inc in next st] 5 times, sc in each of next 3 sts. (48 sc)

Round 9: [Sc in each of next 7 sts, inc in next st] 6 times. (54 sc)

Rounds 10-13: *(4 Rounds)* Sc in each st around. (54 sc)

Round 14: Working in BLO, sc in each st around. (54 sc)

Rounds 15: Sc in each st around. (54 sc)

Alternate rounds, [working 2 rounds in MC, 1 round in **Pattern Stitch***] 7 times.*

Round 16-17: *(2 Rounds)* Sc in each st around. (54 sc)

Round 18: [Sc in each of next 7 sts, sc-dec] 6 times. (48 sc)

Rounds 19-26: *(8 Rounds)* Sc in each st around. (48 sc)

Round 27: [Sc in each of next 6 sts, sc-dec] 6 times. (42 sc)

» Start stuffing Body, adding more as you go.

Rounds 28-30: *(3 Rounds)* Sc in each st around. (42 sc)

Round 31: [Sc in each of next 5 sts, sc-dec] 6 times. (36 sc)

Round 32: Sc in each st around. (36 sc)

Round 33: [Sc in each of next 4 sts, sc-dec] 6 times. (30 sc)

Round 34: Sc in each st around. (30 sc)

Fasten off Color B. Continue in MC.

Round 35: [Sc in each of next 3 sts, sc-dec] 6 times. (24 sc)

Round 36: Hdc in each of next 3 sts, dc in each of next 3 sts, hdc in each of next 3 sts, sc in each of next 15 sts. (24 sts)

Round 37: Sc in each of next 9 sts. Leave remaining sts unworked. Sl st in next st. Fasten off, leaving a long tail for sewing.

Note: *The hdc/dc/hdc-sts on Round 36 will be at the back of the Body and the sc stitches at the front.*

Dress Detail

Round 1: With Neck facing down, working in FLO of Round 13, attach Color C to last st (image 3), ch 2, [3 dc in next st, dc in next st] 27 times; join with sl st to first dc. (108 dc)

Round 2: Ch 2, dc in each st around; fasten off with invisible join. (108 dc) (image 4)

ARM (Make 2)

Rounds 1-3: Using Color A, repeat Rounds 1-3 of Head. At the end of Round 3, there are 18 sc.

Rounds 4-5: *(2 Rounds)* Sc in each st around. (18 sc)

Round 6: [Sc in each of next 4 sts, sc-dec] 3 times. (15 sc)

Round 7: [Sc in each of next 3 sts, sc-dec] 3 times, change to MC. (12 sc) Fasten off Color A.

» Start stuffing Arm, adding more as you go.

Rounds 8-28: *(21 Rounds)* Sc in each st around. (12 sc)

Last Row: Flatten the last round and working through both thicknesses, sc in each of next 6 sc.

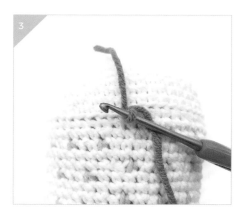

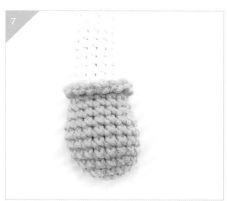

Fasten off and leave a long tail for sewing.

LEG (Make 2)

Rounds 1-3: Using Color B, repeat Rounds 1-3 of Head. At the end of Round 3, there are 18 sc.

Round 4: [Sc in each of next 5 sts, inc in next st] 3 times. (21 sc)

Rounds 5-9: *(5 Rounds)* Sc in each st around. (21 sc)

Round 10: [Sc in each of next 5 sts, sc-dec] 3 times. (18 sc)

Round 11: Sc in each st around. (18 sc)

Round 12: [Sc in each of next 4 sts, sc-dec] 3 times. (15 sc) Change to MC. Leave Color B hanging on the outside (image 5).

» Start stuffing Leg, adding more as you go.

Round 13: Working in BLO, sc in each st around. (15 sc)

Rounds 14-37: *(24 Rounds)* Sc in each st around. (15 sc)

Round 38: [Sc in each of next 3 sts, sc-dec] around. (12 sc)

Round 39: Sc in each st around. (12 sc)

Last Row: Flatten the last round and working through both thicknesses, sc in each of next 6 sc. Fasten off, leaving a long tail for sewing.

Shoe Detail: Working in FLO of Round 12, insert hook in first st and pick up Color B (image 6), [ch 2, sl st in next st] 15 times. Fasten off and weave in ends (image 7).

MANE

Round 1: Using Color C, make a Magic Ring; ch 1, 6 sc in ring, DO NOT JOIN. (6 sc) Tug tail to tighten ring. Mark last stitch.

Round 2: Inc in next st, sc in each of next 5 sts. (7 sc) Move marker each round.

Round 3: Inc in next st, sc in each of next 6 sts. (8 sc)

Round 4: Inc in next st, sc in each of next 7 sts. (9 sc)

Round 5: Inc in next st, sc in each of next 8 sts. (10 sc)

Round 6: Inc in next st, sc in each of next 9 sts. (11 sc)

Round 7: Inc in next st, sc in each of next 10 sts. (12 sc)

Rounds 8-9: *(2 Rounds)* Sc in each st around. (12 sc)

Round 10: [Sc in each of next 2 sts, inc in next st] 4 times. (16 sc)

Rounds 11-12: *(2 Rounds)* Sc in each st around. (16 sc)

Round 13: [Sc in each of next 2 sts, sc-dec] 4 times. (12 sc)

Rounds 14-17: *(4 Rounds)* Sc in each st around. (12 sc)

Round 18: [Sc in next st, sc-dec] 4 times. (8 sc)

Round 19: Sc in each st around. (8 sc) Fasten off and close remaining sts, leaving a long tail for sewing.

TAIL

Rounds 1-7: Using Color A, repeat Rounds 1-7 of Mane. At the end of Round 7, there are 12 sc.

Round 8: Inc in next st, sc in each of next 11 sts. (13 sc)

Round 9: Inc in next st, sc in each of next 12 sts. (14 sc)

Round 10: Inc in next st, sc in each of next 13 sts. (15 sc)

Rounds 11-12: *(2 Rounds)* Sc in each st around. (15 sc)

Round 13: [Sc in each of next 4 sts, inc in next st] 3 times. (18 sc)

Rounds 14-15: *(2 Rounds)* Sc in each st around. (18 sc)

» Start stuffing Tail lightly, adding more as you go.

Round 16: [Sc in each of next 4 sts, sc-dec] 3 times. (15 sc)

Rounds 17-18: *(2 Rounds)* Sc in each st around. (15 sc)

Round 19: [Sc in each of next 3 sts, sc-dec] 3 times. (12 sc)

Rounds 20-21: *(2 Rounds)* Sc in each st around. (12 sc)

Round 22: [Sc in each of next 4 sts, sc-dec] 2 times. (10 sc)

Last Row: Flatten the last round and working through both thicknesses, sc in each of next 5 sc.

Fasten off, leaving a long tail for sewing.

EAR (Make 2)

Round 1: Using MC, make a Magic Ring; ch 1, 6 sc in ring, DO NOT JOIN. (6 sc) Tug tail to tighten ring. Mark last stitch.

Round 2: [Inc in next st, sc in next st] 3 times. (9 sc) Move marker each round.

Round 3: [Sc in each of next 2 sts, inc in next st] 3 times. (12 sc)

Round 4: [Sc in each of next 3 sts, inc in next st] 3 times. (15 sc)

Round 5: Sc in each st around. (15 sc)

Round 6: [Sc in each of next 4 sts, inc in next st] 3 times. (18 sc)

Round 7: Sc in each st around. (18 sc)

Round 8: [Sc in each of next 5 sts, inc in next st] 3 times. (21 sc)

Round 9: Sc in each st around. (21 sc)

Round 10: [Sc in each of next 5 sts, sc-dec] 3 times. (18 sc)

Rounds 11-12: *(2 Rounds)* Sc in each st around. (18 sc)

Round 13: [Sc in each of next 4 sts, sc-dec] 3 times. (15 sc)

Round 14: Sc in each st around. (15 sc)

Round 15: [Sc in each of next 3 sts, sc-dec] 3 times. (12 sc)

Round 16: Sc in each st around. (12 sc) Sl st in next st. Fasten off, leaving a long tail for sewing.

COLLAR

Row 1: Using Color C, ch 45; starting in the third ch from hook, 3 dc in each of next 5 ch; change to Color B, 3 dc in each of next 38 ch. Fasten off, leaving a long tail for sewing (image 8).

» Roll the beginning of Row 1 to form a flower. Using Color C tail, sew the flower to secure (images 9, 10 & 11), making sure the remainder of the row fits around the neck.

FLOWER (Make 2)

Using Lime Juice, ch 27, starting in the third ch from hook, [3 dc in next ch, sc in next ch] 5 times; change to Lemon Chiffon, [3 dc in each of next 2 ch, sc in next ch] 5 times. Fasten off, leaving a long tail for sewing.

» Roll the flower into shape and using long tail, sew to secure (image 12).

Repeat Flower using Bluebell and Baby Blue (image 13).

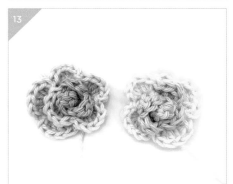
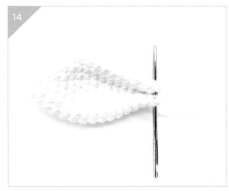
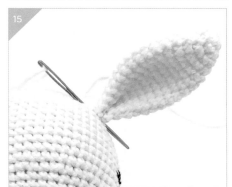
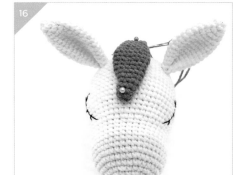

ASSEMBLY - Use photos as guide

Head - Mark the 25th st of Round 15 with a pin. This is the center front of head.

Ears - Using long tail and yarn needle, fold the last round of Ear in half, and sew edges together (image 14). Repeat for other Ear. Position Ears on either side of Head between Rounds 28 & 30, about 12 stitches apart and sew in place (image 15).

Mane - Position Mane between the Ears, from Rounds 18 & 35, and sew in place (image 16).

Eyes - Using Cotton Thread, embroider Sleeping Eyes. Start the front corners between Rounds 15 & 16 and the back corners between Rounds 22 & 23. Embroider Eyelashes (images 17).

Flowers - Position and sew the Flowers on Head (image 18).

Face - Using a small makeup brush, apply blusher to the cheeks and the inside of Ears.

Body - Position and sew the Body to Rounds 23 & 30 of the Head, positioning the back of the body towards the back of the head, stuffing firmly before closing.

Arms - Position the Arms on either side of the Body (2 rounds below Neck). Using long tails and yarn needle, sew them in place.

Legs - Position the Legs on either side of the Body at Round 9. Using long tails and yarn needle, sew them in place.

Tail - Sew Tail to center back of Body, at Rounds 8 & 11 (image 19).

Collar - Position and pin the Flower on Neck. Wrap Collar around Neck and sew in place (images 20, 21, 22 & 23).

Titou The Tiger

Titou, the little tiger loves exploring the jungle and taking his friends on expeditions. He knows of many beautiful places, where one can be at peace and relax. Let's follow him!

MATERIALS

Scheepjes Softfun

Main Color (MC): Mustard (2621)
Color A: Brown (2623)
Color B: Dark Red (2617)
Color C: Cream (2426)

Size C-2 (2.75 mm) Crochet Hook - or size suitable for yarn used
Yarn Needle

Stitch Markers
⁵⁄₁₆" (8 mm) Safety Eyes - 2
Small Button - 1
Small piece of fabric - 1¾" (4.5 cm) wide by ½" (1.5 cm) long (for Patch)
Thread and needle - for sewing on button & fabric
Toy Stuffing
Cosmetic Blusher & Brush - for Cheeks

Finished Size
About 7⅞" (20 cm) tall

Skill Level
♥ ♥

HEAD

Note: *The colored font indicates where Color A is used. Use the Cut & Tie Method for the color changes.*

Round 1: Using MC, make a Magic Ring; ch 1, 8 sc in ring, DO NOT JOIN. (8 sc) Tug tail to tighten ring. Mark last stitch.

Round 2: Inc in each st around. (16 sc) Move marker each round.

Round 3: [Sc in next st, inc in next st] 8 times. (24 sc)

Round 4: [Sc in each of next 2 sts, inc in next st] 8 times. (32 sc)

Round 5: [Sc in each of next 3 sts, inc in next st] 3 times, sc in each of next 2 sts; change to Color A, sc in next st, inc in next st, sc in each of next 3 sts, inc in next st, sc in next st; change to MC, sc in each of next 2 sts, inc in next st, [sc in each of next 3 sts, inc in next st] 2 times. (40 sc)

Round 6: Sc in next st, inc in next st, [sc in each of next 4 sts, inc in next st] 7 times, sc in each of next 3 sts. (48 sc)

Round 7: Sc in each st around. (48 sc)

Round 8: Sc in each of next 20 sts; change to Color A, sc in each of next 12 sts; change to MC, sc in each of next 16 sts. (48 sc)

Round 9: Sc in each st around. (48 sc)

Round 10: [Sc in each of next 5 sts, inc in next st] 8 times. (56 sc)

Round 11: Sc in each of next 25 sts; change to Color A, sc in each of next 10 sts; change to MC, sc in each of next 21 sts. (56 sc)

Rounds 12-14: *(3 Rounds)* Sc in each st around. (56 sc)

Round 15: Change to color A, [sc in each of next 6 sts, inc in next st] 3 times; change to MC, [sc in each of next 6 sts, inc in next st] 2 times, sc in each of next 5 sts; change to Color A, sc in next st, inc in next st, [sc in each of next 6 sts, inc in next st] 2 times, change to MC. (64 sc)

Rounds 16-17: *(2 Rounds)* Sc in each st around. (64 sc)

Round 18: Change to color A, sc in each of next 24 sts; change to MC, sc in each of next 21 sts; change to Color A, sc in each of next 19 sts, change to MC. (64 sc)

Round 19: Sc in each st around. (64 sc)

Round 20: [Sc in each of next 15 sts, inc in next st] 4 times. (68 sc)

Round 21: Change to color A, sc in each of next 15 sts, **sc-dec**, sc in each of next 8 sts; change to MC, sc in each of next 7 sts, sc-dec, sc in each of next 13 sts; change to color A, sc in each of next 2 sts, sc-dec, sc in each of next 15 sts, sc-dec; change to MC. (64 sc) Fasten off Color A.

Round 22: [Sc in each of next 6 sts, sc-dec] 8 times. (56 sc)

» Insert Safety Eyes in the MC section between Rounds 16 & 17, about 11 stitches apart.

Round 23: Sc in each of next 3 sts, sc-dec, [sc in each of next 5 sts, sc-dec] 7 times, sc in each of next 2 sts. (48 sc)

Round 24: [Sc in each of next 4 sts, sc-dec] 8 times. (40 sc)

Round 25: Sc in next st, sc-dec, [sc in each of next 3 sts, sc-dec] 7 times, sc in each of next 2 sts. (32 sc)

Round 26: [Sc in each of next 2 sts, sc-dec] 8 times. (24 sc).

Round 27: Sc in each st around. (24 sc). Sl st in next st. Fasten off, leaving a long tail for sewing.

» Stuff Head firmly.

EAR (Make 2)

Note: *The colored font indicates where Color C is used. Use the Stranding Method for the color changes.*

Rounds 1-2: Using Color A, repeat Rounds 1-2 of Head. At the end of Round 2, change to MC. (16 sc). Fasten off Color A.

Round 3: Sc in each of next 7 sts; change to Color C, sc in each of next 2 sts; change to MC, sc in each of next 7 sts. (16 sc)

Rounds 4-5: *(2 Rounds)* Sc in each of next 6 sts; change to Color C, sc in each of next 4 sts; change to MC, sc in each of next 6 sts. (16 sc)

Round 6: Sc in each of next 2 sts, sc-dec, sc in each of next 2 sts; change to Color C, sc-dec, sc in each of next 2 sts; change to MC, sc-dec, sc in each of next 2 sts, sc-dec. (12 sc) Sl st in next st. Fasten off, leaving a long tail of MC for sewing.

MUZZLE

Rounds 1-2: Using Color C, repeat Rounds 1-2 of Head. At the end of Round 2, there are 16 sc.

Round 3: Sc in each of next 3 sts, inc in each of next 2 sts, sc in each of next 6 sts, inc in each of next 2 sts, sc in each of next 3 sts. (20 sc) Sl st in next st. Fasten off, leaving a long tail for sewing.

HEAD ASSEMBLY (use photos as guide)

Muzzle - Using Color A, embroider a Nose on Muzzle (image 1 - Muzzle and Ears). Position Muzzle between the Eyes and sew in place (image 2).

Ears - Position Ears on either side of Head (between Rounds 6 & 10) and sew in place (images 3 & 4).

ARM (Make 2)

Round 1: Using MC, make a Magic Ring; ch 1, 8 sc in ring, DO NOT JOIN. (8 sc) Tug tail to tighten ring. Mark last stitch.

Round 2: [Sc in next st, inc in next st] 4 times. (12 sc) Move marker each round.

Round 3: [Sc in each of next 5 sts, inc in next st] 2 times. (14 sc)

Rounds 4-7: *(4 Rounds)* Sc in each st around. (14 sc) At the end of Round 7, change to Color B. Fasten off MC.

Round 8: Sc in each st around. (14 sc)

Round 9: Working in BLO, sc in each st around. (14 sc)

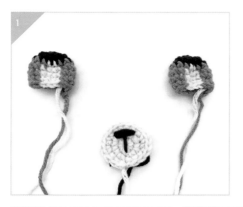

Rounds 10-16: *(7 Rounds)* Sc in each st around. (14 sc)

» Stuff Arm lightly.

Round 17: [Sc in each of next 5 sts, sc-dec] 2 times. (12 sc)

Last Row: Flatten the last round and working through both thicknesses, sc in each of next 6 sc. Fasten off, leaving a long tail for sewing.

Arm Detail: Working in FLO of Round 8, attach Color B (image 5), sl st in each st around. Fasten off and weave in ends.

(Image 6 - Arms & Tail)

Tail

Rounds 1-2: Using MC, repeat Rounds 1-2 of Arms.
At the end of Round 2, change to Color A. (12 sc)

Round 3: [Sc in each of next 5 sts, inc in next st] 2 times, change to MC. (14 sc)
Alternate 2 rounds MC and 1 round Color A.

Rounds 4-16: *(13 Rounds)* Sc in each st around. (14 sc)

Round 17: [Sc in each of next 5 sts, sc-dec] 2 times. (12 sc)

Rounds 18-22: *(5 Rounds)* Sc in each st around. (12 sc)
At the end of Round 22, fasten off Color A. Continue with MC.

» Stuff Tail lightly.

Last Row: Flatten the last round and working through both thicknesses, sc in each of next 6 sc. Fasten off, leaving a long tail for sewing.

LEGS

First Leg

Rounds 1-4: Using Color A, repeat Rounds 1-4 of Head.
At the end of Round 4, there are 32 sc.

Round 5: Sc in each st around. (32 sc)

Round 6: Sc in each of next 8 sts, [sc-dec] 8 times, sc in each of next 8 sts. (24 sc)

Round 7: Sc in each st around. (24 sc)

Round 8: Sc in each of next 6 sts, [sc in next st, sc-dec] 4 times, sc in each of next 6 sts. (20 sc)

Round 9: Sc in each st around. (20 sc) Change to MC. Leave Color A hanging on the outside (image 7).

Round 10: Working in BLO, sc in each st around. (20 sc) Fasten off.

» *Mark the 13th st of Round 10 (on First Leg only - for Joining Legs).*

Leg Detail

Working in FLO of Round 9, insert hook in first st and pick up Color A (image 8), sl st in each st around. Fasten off and weave in ends (image 9).

Second Leg

Rounds 1-10: Repeat Rounds 1-10 of First Leg.
Round 11: Sc in each of next 8 sts. Leave remaining sts unworked. Do not fasten off.

» Repeat Leg Detail on Second Leg.

BODY

Round 1: *(Joining Legs)* Working on Second Leg, ch 4; working on First Leg, sc in marked st (image 10), sc in each of next 19 sts; working in ch-4, sc in each of next 4 ch; working on Second Leg, sc in each of next 20 sts; working in unused loops on other side of ch-4, sc in each of next 4 ch. (48 sc) Mark last st made. Move marker each round.
Round 2: Sc in each st around, change to Color A. (48 sc)
Round 3: Sc in each of next 40 sts, [sc in next st, inc in next st] 4 times, change to MC. (52 sc)
Round 4: [Sc in next st, inc in next st] 2 times, sc in each of next 48 sts. (54 sc)
Round 5: Sc in each st around, change to Color A. (54 sc)
Round 6: Sc in each st around, change to Color B. (54 sc) Fasten off Color A and MC.
Round 7: Sc in each st around. (54 sc)
Round 8: Working in BLO, sc in each st around. (54 sc)
Round 9: Sc in each st around. (54 sc)

» Start stuffing Legs and Body firmly, adding more as you go.

Round 10: [Sc in each of next 7 sts, sc-dec] 6 times. (48 sc)
Rounds 11-14: *(4 Rounds)* Sc in each st around. (48 sc)
Round 15: [Sc in each of next 6 sts, sc-dec] 6 times. (42 sc)
Rounds 16-19: *(4 Rounds)* Sc in each st around. (42 sc)
Round 20: [Sc in each of next 5 sts, sc-dec] 6 times. (36 sc)
Rounds 21-23: *(3 Rounds)* Sc in each st around. (36 sc)
Round 24: [Sc in each of next 4 sts, sc-dec] 6 times. (30 sc)
Round 25: Sc in each st around. (30 sc)
Round 26: [Sc in each of next 3 sts, sc-dec] 6 times. (24 sc)
Sl st in next st. Fasten off, leaving a long tail for sewing.

Sweater Detail

Working in the FLO of Round 7, attach Color B to first st (image 11); sl st in each st around. Fasten off and weave in ends.

COLLAR

Using Color B, ch 40, starting in the third ch from hook, dc in each ch across. (38 dc) Fasten off, leaving a long tail for sewing (image 12).

BODY ASSEMBLY (use photos as guide)

Tail - Position and sew the Tail to center back of Body, 1 round below Sweater Detail (image 13).

Arms - Position the Arms on either side of the Body (2 rounds below the last round). Using long tails and yarn needle, sew them in place.

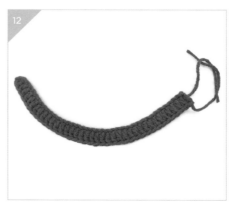

Head - Sew the Head to Body, stuffing firmly before closing (image 14).

Collar & Patch - Wrap the Collar around Neck, overlapping the ends. Sew a button to secure the ends. Position and sew Fabric Patch to front of Sweater (image 15).

Face - Using a small makeup brush, apply blusher to the cheeks.

Toto Racoon

Toto is an active chap and loves sports. Every morning, he gets up early to go jogging in the forest - no matter what the weather is like. This morning it's a little bit chilly outside, so he's wearing his favorite sweater.

MATERIALS

Scheepjes Softfun

Main Color (MC): Dark Grey (2510)
Color A: Black Grey (2532)
Color B: Cream (2426)
Color C: Olive Green (2616)
Color D: Mustard (2621)
Color E: White (2412)

Size C-2 (2.75 mm) Crochet Hook - or size suitable for yarn used
Yarn Needle
Embroidery Needle
Stitch Markers
⅜" (8 mm) Safety Eyes - 2
Toy Stuffing
Cosmetic Blusher & Brush - for Cheeks

Finished Size
About 7⅞" (20 cm) tall

Skill Level
♥♥♥

HEAD

Note: *The colored font indicates where Color A is used. Use the Cut & Tie Method for the color changes.*

Round 1: Using MC, make a Magic Ring; ch 1, 8 sc in ring, DO NOT JOIN. (8 sc) Tug tail to tighten ring. Mark last stitch.

Round 2: Inc in each st around. (16 sc) Move marker each round.

Round 3: [Sc in next st, inc in next st] 8 times. (24 sc)

Round 4: [Sc in each of next 2 sts, inc in next st] around. (32 sc)

Round 5: Sc in next st, inc in next st, [sc in each of next 3 sts, inc in next st] 7 times, sc in each of next 2 sts. (40 sc)

Round 6: [Sc in each of next 4 sts, inc in next st] 8 times. (48 sc)

Rounds 7-10: *(4 Rounds)* Sc in each st around. (48 sc)

Round 11: [Sc in each of next 7 sts, inc in next st] 6 times. (54 sc)

Round 12: Sc in each st around. (54 sc)

Round 13: Sc in each of next 12 sts, inc in next st, sc in each of next 26 sts, inc in next st, sc in each of next 14 sts. (56 sc)

Round 14: Sc in each of next 12 sts, inc in each of next 2 sts, sc in each of next 3 sts; change to Color A, sc in each of next 5 sts; change to MC, sc in each of next 10 sts; change to Color A, sc in each of next 5 sts; change to MC, sc in each of next 3 sts, inc in each of next 2 sts, sc in each of next 14 sts. (60 sc)

Round 15: Sc in each of next 13 sts, inc in each of next 2 sts, sc in each of next 3 sts; change to Color A, sc in each of next 7 sts; change to MC, sc in each of next 8 sts; change to Color A, sc in each of next 7 sts; change to MC, sc in each of next 3 sts, inc in each of next 2 sts, sc in each of next 15 sts. (64 sc)

Round 16: Sc in each of next 14 sts, inc in next st, sc in each of next 4 sts; change to Color A, sc in each of next 24 sts; change to MC, sc in each of next 4 sts, inc in next st, sc in each of next 16 sts. (66 sc)

Round 17: Sc in each of next 14 sts, **sc-dec**, sc in each of next 4 sts; change to Color A, sc in each of next 24 sts; change to MC, sc in each of next 4 sts, sc-dec, sc in each of next 16 sts. (64 sc) Fasten off Color A.

Round 18: Sc in each of next 13 sts, [sc-dec] 3 times, sc in each of next 24 sts, [sc-dec] 3 times, sc in each of next 15 sts. (58 sc)

Round 19: Sc in each of next 12 sts, [sc-dec] 2 times, sc in each of next 24 sts, [sc-dec] 2 times, sc in each of next 14 sts. (54 sc)

» Insert Safety Eyes in the Color A section between Rounds 15 & 16, about 12 stitches apart.

Round 20: [Sc in each of next 7 sts, sc-dec] 6 times. (48 sc)

Round 21: Sc in each of next 3 sts, sc-dec, [sc in each of next 6 sts, sc-dec] 5 times, sc in each of next 3 sts. (42 sc)

Round 22: [Sc in each of next 5 sts, sc-dec] 6 times. (36 sc)

Round 23: Sc in each of next 2 sts, sc-dec, [sc in each of next 4 sts, sc-dec] 5 times, sc in each of next 2 sts. (30 sc)

Round 24: [Sc in each of next 3 sts, sc-dec] 6 times. (24 sc)

Round 25: Sc in each st around. (24 sc) Sl st in next st to fasten off, leaving a long tail for sewing.

» Stuff the Head firmly.

SNOUT

Round 1: Using Color B, make a Magic Ring; ch 1, 6 sc in ring, DO NOT JOIN. (6 sc) Tug tail to tighten ring. Mark last stitch.

Round 2: [Inc in next st, sc in next st] 3 times. (9 sc) Move marker each round.

Round 3: [Inc in next st, sc in each of next 2 sts] 3 times. (12 sc)

Round 4: [Inc in next st, sc in each of next 3 sts] 3 times. (15 sc)

Round 5: [Inc in next st, sc in each of next 4 sts] 3 times. (18 sc) Sl st in next st. Fasten off, leaving a long tail for sewing.

» Using Color A, embroider a Nose on Snout (images 1, 2, 3, 4 & 5).

EAR (Make 2)

Note: *The colored font indicates where Color B is used. Use the Stranding Method for the color changes.*

Rounds 1-3: Using Color A, repeat Rounds 1-3 of Snout. At the end of Round 3, change to MC. (12 sc) Fasten off Color A.

Round 4: Sc in each of next 5 st; change to Color B, inc in each of next 2 st; change to MC, sc in each of next 5 sts. (14 sc)

Round 5: Sc in each of next 3 sts, inc in next st, sc in next st; change to Color B, sc in each of next 4 sts; change to MC, sc in next st, inc in next st, sc in each of next 3 sts. (16 sc)

Round 6: Sc in each of next 4 sts, inc in next st, sc in next st; change to Color B, inc in next st, sc in each of next 2 sts, inc in next st; change to MC, sc in next st, inc in next st, sc in each of next 4 sts. (20 sc)

Round 7: Sc in each of next 7 sts; change to Color B, sc in each of next 6 sts; change to MC, sc in each of next 7 sts. (20 sc) Fasten off Color B. Sl st in next st. Fasten off MC, leaving a long tail for sewing.

HEAD ASSEMBLY (use photos as guide)

Eyebrows - Using Color B, embroider a straight stitch, two rounds above each Eye (image 6).

Snout - Position Snout between the Eyes and sew in place, stuffing lightly before closing (image 7).

Ears - Position Ears on either side of Head (between Rounds 3 & 9) and sew in place (images 8 & 9).

(image - Arms & Tail)

ARM (Make 2)

Note: *Arms are not stuffed.*

Round 1: Using MC, make a Magic Ring; ch 1, 6 sc in ring, DO NOT JOIN. (6 sc) Tug tail to tighten ring. Mark last stitch.

Round 2: [Inc in next st, sc in next st] 3 times. (9 sc) Move marker each round.

Round 3: Sc in each st around. (9 sc)

Round 4: [Sc-dec, sc in next st] 3 times, change to Color D. (6 sc) Fasten off MC.

Round 5: Inc in each st around. (12 sc)

Rounds 6-11: *(6 Rounds)* Sc in each st around. (12 sc) At the end of Round 11, change to Color E.

Round 12: Sc in each st around, change to Color C. (12 sc)

Round 13: Sc in each st around, change to Color E. (12 sc)

Round 14: Sc in each st around, change to Color D. (12 sc) Fasten off Color C & Color E.

Rounds 15-16: *(2 Rounds)* Sc in each st around. (12 sc)

Last Row: Flatten the last round and working through both thicknesses, sc in each of next 6 sc. Fasten off, leaving a long tail for sewing.

TAIL

Round 1: Using Color A, make a Magic Ring; ch 1, 6 sc in ring, DO NOT JOIN. (6 sc) Tug tail to tighten ring. Mark last stitch.

Round 2: [Inc in next st, sc in each of next 2 sts] 2 times. (8 sc) Move marker each round.

Round 3: [Sc in next st, inc in next st] 4 times, change to Color B. (12 sc)
Alternate Color B and Color A every 3 rounds.

Round 4: [Sc in each of next 5 sts, inc in next st] 2 times. (14 sc)

Rounds 5-9: *(5 Rounds)* Sc in each st around. (14 sc)

» Start stuffing Tail, adding more as you go.

Round 10: [Sc in each of next 5 sts, sc-dec] 2 times. (12 sc)
Rounds 11-12: *(2 Rounds)* Sc in each st around. (12 sc)
Round 13: [Sc in each of next 4 sts, sc-dec] 2 times. (10 sc)
Round 14: Sc in each st around. (10 sc)
Round 15: Sc in each of next 8 sts, sc-dec. (9 sc)
Round 16: Sc in each st around. (9 sc)
Round 17: Sc in each of next 7 sts, sc-dec. (8 sc)
Round 18: Sc in each of next 6 sts, sc-dec. (7 sc)
Round 19: Sc in each st around. (7 sc)
Fasten off, leaving a long tail of Color A for sewing.

LEGS

First Leg

Rounds 1-2: Using Color A, repeat Rounds 1-2 of Head. At the end of Round 2, there are 16 sc.
Round 3: Sc in next st, inc in next st, sc in each of next 4 sts, inc in each of next 4 sts, sc in each of next 4 sts, inc in next st, sc in last st. (22 sc)
Rounds 4-6: *(3 Rounds)* Sc in each st around. (22 sc)
Round 7: Sc in each of next 7 sts, [sc-dec] 4 times, sc in each of next 7 sts. (18 sc)
Round 8: Sc in each of next 5 sts, [sc-dec] 4 times, sc in each of next 5 sts. (14 sc) Change to Color C. Leave Color A hanging on the outside (image 10).
Round 9: Working in BLO, sc in each st around. (14 sc)
Round 10: Sc in each of next 3 sts, inc in next st, sc in each of next 6 sts, inc in next st, sc in each of next 3 sts. (16 sc)
Round 11: Sc in each st around. (16 sc)
Round 12: [Sc in each of next 7 sts, inc in next st] 2 times. (18 sc)
Rounds 13-14: *(2 Rounds)* Sc in each st around. (18 sc)
Round 15: Sc in each of next 4 sts, inc in next st, sc in each of next 8 sts, inc in next st, sc in each of next 4 sts. (20 sc)
Rounds 16-17: *(2 Rounds)* Sc in each st around. (20 sc)
Round 18: Sc in each of next 14 sts. Leave remaining sts unworked. Fasten off.

» Stuff Leg firmly.

Leg Detail

Working in FLO of Round 8, insert hook in first st and pick up Color A (image 11), sl st in each st around. Fasten off and weave in ends.

Second Leg

Rounds 1-17: Repeat Rounds 1-17 of First Leg.
Round 18: Sc in each st around. (20 sc)
Round 19: Sc in each of next 6 sts. Leave remaining sts unworked. Do not fasten off.

» Repeat Leg Detail on Second Leg (image 12).

BODY

Round 1: *(Joining Legs)* Working on Second Leg, ch 2; working on First Leg, sc in last st made (image 13), sc in each of next 19 sts; working in ch-2, sc in each of next 2 ch; working on Second Leg, sc in each of next 20 sts; working in unused loops on other side of ch-2, sc in each of next 2 ch. (44 sc) Mark last st made. Move marker each round.
Round 2: [Sc in each of next 10 sts, inc in next st] 4 times. (48 sc)
Rounds 3-4: *(2 Rounds)* Sc in each st around. (48 sc) At the end of Round 4, change to Color D. Fasten off Color C.
Round 5: Sc in each st around. (48 sc)
Round 6: Working in BLO, [sc in each of next 6 st, sc-dec] 6 times. (42 sc)
Rounds 7-10: *(4 Rounds)* Sc in each st around. (42 sc)

» Start stuffing Body firmly, adding more as you go.

Round 11: [Sc in each of next 5 sts, sc-dec] 6 times. (36 sc)
Rounds 12-13: *(2 Rounds)* Sc in each st around, change to Color E. (36 sc)
Round 14: Sc in each st around, change to Color C. (36 sc)
Round 15: Sc in each st around, change to Color E. (36 sc)
Round 16: Sc in each st around, change to Color D. (36 sc) Fasten off Color C & Color E.
Round 17: Sc in each st around. (36 sc)
Round 18: [Sc in each of next 4 sts, sc-dec] 6 times. (30 sc)
Round 19: Sc in each st around. (30 sc)
Round 20: Working in BLO *(of Round 19)*, [sc in each of next 3 sts, sc-dec] 6 times. (24 sc)

Round 21: *(Collar)* Working in FLO *(of Round 20)*, ch 2, [hdc in each of next 3 sts, 2 hdc in next st] 6 times; join with sl st to first hdc. (30 hdc)

Round 22: Ch 2, hdc in same st as joining, hdc in next 2 st, 2 hdc in next st, [hdc in each of next 4 sts, 2 hdc in next st] 5 times, hdc in each of next 2 sts; fasten off with invisible join. (36 hdc)

Sweater Detail

With feet facing upwards, working in FLO of Round 5, attach Color D to first st (image 14), ch 1, sc in each st around; fasten off with invisible join. (48 sc) (image 15).

Sweater Ties

Using Color D, ch 8 (image 16); working in FLO of Round 19, starting at center front, (image 17), sl st in each st around; ch 6. Fasten off (image 18).

BODY ASSEMBLY (use photos as guide)

Arms - Position the Arms on either side of the Body (below the Ties). Using long tails and yarn needle, sew them in place (image 19).

Tail - Position and sew the Tail to center back of Body, below Sweater Detail (image 20).

Head - Sew the Head to BLO of Round 20 of Body, stuffing firmly before closing (image 21).

Face - Using a small makeup brush, apply blusher to the cheeks.

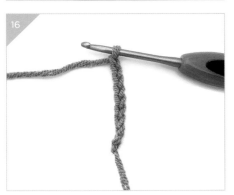

Vivi The Bunny

It's Springtime - Vivi's favorite season of the year. The forest comes alive with color - all the different shades of green for the new leaves on the trees, not to mention all the hues of the blossoming flowers. Vivi is in her element!

MATERIALS

Scheepjes Catona Denim

Color A: Light Yellow (120)
(plus a small amount for Flowers)

Scheepjes Catona

Main Color (MC): Snow White (106)
Color B: Green Yellow (245)
Color C: Kiwi (205)
Old Rose (408), Powder Pink (238) &
Baby Blue (509) - small amounts for
Flowers

**Scheepjes Maxi Sweet Treat
(Cotton Thread)**

Black Coffee (162) - for Eyes

Sizes B-1 (2.25 mm) (Main Hook) & C-2
(2.75 mm) (for Shorts)
Crochet Hooks - or sizes
suitable for yarn used
(Use Main Hook throughout,
unless otherwise stated.)
Yarn Needle
Embroidery Needle
Stitch Markers
Toy Stuffing
Cosmetic Blusher & Brush - for
Cheeks & Ears

Finished Size
About 11" (28 cm) tall

Skill Level
♥ ♥ ♥

HEAD & BODY

Round 1: Starting at Head, using MC, make a Magic Ring; ch 1, 8 sc in ring, DO NOT JOIN. (8 sc) Tug tail to tighten ring. Mark last stitch.
Round 2: Inc in each st around. (16 sc) Move marker each round.
Round 3: [Sc in next st, inc in next st] 8 times. (24 sc)
Round 4: [Sc in each of next 2 sts, inc in next st] 8 times. (32 sc)
Round 5: [Sc in each of next 3 sts, inc in next st] 8 times. (40 sc)
Round 6: Sc in each st around. (40 sc)
Round 7: [Sc in each of next 4 sts, inc in next st] 8 times. (48 sc)
Rounds 8-11: *(4 Rounds)* Sc in each st around. (48 sc)
Round 12: [Sc in each of next 7 sts, inc in next st] 6 times. (54 sc)
Rounds 13-15: *(3 Rounds)* Sc in each st around. (54 sc)
Round 16: [Sc in each of next 8 sts, inc in next st] 6 times. (60 sc)
Round 17: [Sc in each of next 9 sts, inc in next st] 6 times. (66 sc)
Round 18: [Sc in each of next 9 sts, **sc-dec**] 6 times. (60 sc)
Round 19: Sc in each of next 4 sts, sc-dec, [sc in each of next 8 sts, sc-dec] 5 times, sc in each of next 4 sts. (54 sc)
Round 20: [Sc in each of next 7 sts, sc-dec] 6 times. (48 sc)
Round 21: Sc in each of next 3 sts, sc-dec, [sc in each of next 6 sts, sc-dec] 5 times, sc in each of next 3 sts. (42 sc)
Round 22: [Sc in each of next 5 sts, sc-dec] 6 times. (36 sc)
Round 23: Sc in each of next 2 sts, sc-dec, [sc in each of next 4 sts, sc-dec] 5 times, sc in each of next 2 sts. (30 sc)
Round 24: [Sc in each of next 3 sts, sc-dec] 6 times, change to Color A. (24 sc) Fasten off MC.

» Stuff Head firmly, but not the part of Neck.

Round 25: [Sc in each of next 3 sts, inc in next st] 6 times. (30 sc)
Rounds 26-30: *(5 Rounds)* Sc in each st around. (30 sc)
Round 31: [Sc in each of next 5 sts, inc in next st] 5 times. (35 sc)
Rounds 32-34: *(3 Rounds)* Sc in each st around. (35 sc)
Round 35: [Sc in each of next 6 sts, inc in next st] 5 times. (40 sc)

» Start stuffing Neck and Body firmly, adding more as you go.

Rounds 36-38: *(3 Rounds)* Sc in each st around. (40 sc)
Round 39: [Sc in each of next 7 sts, inc in next st] 5 times. (45 sc)
Rounds 40-41: *(2 Rounds)* Sc in each st around. (45 sc)
Round 42: [Sc in each of next 7 sts, sc-dec] 5 times. (40 sc)
Round 43: Sc in each st around. (40 sc)
Round 44: [Sc in each of next 3 sts, sc-dec] 8 times. (32 sc)
Round 45: [Sc in each of next 2 sts, sc-dec] 8 times. (24 sc)
Round 46: [Sc in next st, sc-dec] 8 times. (16 sc)

Round 47: [Sc-dec] 8 times. (8 sc)

» Finish stuffing Body.

Fasten off and close remaining sts, weaving in end.

EAR (Make 2)

Round 1: Using MC, make a Magic Ring; ch 1, 6 sc in ring, DO NOT JOIN. (6 sc) Tug tail to tighten ring. Mark last stitch.
Round 2: [Inc in next st, sc in next st] 3 times. (9 sc) Move marker each round.
Round 3: [Sc in each of next 2 sts, inc in next st] 3 times. (12 sc)
Round 4: Sc in each st around. (12 sc)
Round 5: [Sc in each of next 2 sts, inc in next st] 4 times. (16 sc)
Round 6: [Sc in each of next 3 sts, inc in next st] 4 times. (20 sc)
Rounds 7-13: *(7 Rounds)* Sc in each st around. (20 sc)
Round 14: [Sc in each of next 8 sts, sc-dec] 2 times. (18 sc)
Rounds 15-16: *(2 Rounds)* Sc in each st around. (18 sc)
Round 17: [Sc in each of next 7 sts, sc-dec] 2 times. (16 sc)
Rounds 18-19: *(2 Rounds)* Sc in each st around. (16 sc)
Round 20: [Sc in each of next 6 sts, sc-dec] 2 times. (14 sc)
Round 21: Sc in each st around. (14 sc) Sl st in next st.
Fasten off, leaving a long tail for sewing.

ARM (Make 2)

Note: *Arms are not stuffed.*
Round 1: Using MC, make a Magic Ring; ch 1, 8 sc in ring, DO NOT JOIN. (8 sc) Tug tail to tighten ring. Mark last stitch, move the marker each round.
Rounds 2-19: *(18 Rounds)* Sc in each st around. (8 sc)

Last Row: Flatten the last round and working through both thicknesses, sc in each of next 4 sc.
Fasten off, leaving a long tail for sewing.

LEG (Make 2)

Rounds 1-2: Using Color B, repeat Rounds 1-2 of Head & Body.
At the end of Round 2, there are 16 sc.
Round 3: Sc in next st, inc in next st, sc in each of next 4 sts, inc in each of next 4 sts, sc in each of next 4 sts, inc in next st, sc in last st. (22 sc)
Rounds 4-6: *(3 Rounds)* Sc in each st around. (22 sc)
Round 7: Sc in each of next 7 sts, [sc-dec] 4 times, sc in each of next 7 sts. (18 sc)
Round 8: Sc in each st around. (18 sc)
Round 9: Sc in each of next 5 sts, [sc-dec] 4 times, sc in each of next 5 sts. (14 sc)
Round 10: Sc in each of next 6 sts, sc-dec, sc in each of next 6 sts. (13 sc)
Rounds 11-13: *(3 Rounds)* Sc in each st around. (13 sc)

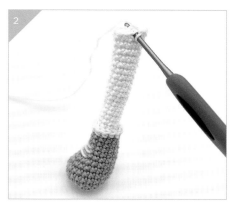

At the end of the Round 13, change to MC. Fasten off Color B.

» Start stuffing Leg firmly, adding more as you go.

Round 14: Working in BLO, [sc in each of next 2 sts, sc-dec] 3 times, sc in last st. (10 sc)

Note: *I prefer to work the Shoe Detail at this point, before continuing with the Leg.*

Rounds 15-30: *(16 Rounds)* Sc in each st around. (10 sc)
Round 31: Sc in each st around ending at center back of Leg, adding additional sc-sts if needed (image 1).

Last Row: Flatten the last round and working through both thicknesses, sc in each of next 5 sc (image 2). Fasten off, leaving a long tail for sewing.

Shoe Detail: Working in the FLO of Round 13, attach Color A to the last st (image 3), ch 1, sc in each st around; fasten off with invisible join, leaving a long tail.

» Using long tail, embroider small lines across front of Shoe (images 4 & 5). Weave in ends (image 6).

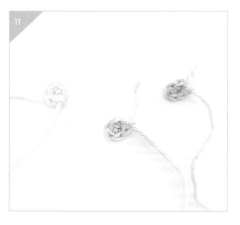

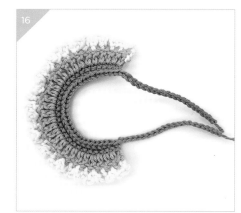

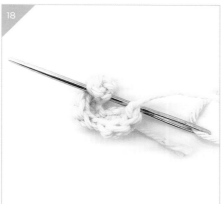

SHORTS

Pants Leg (Make 2)

Round 1: Using Color C and larger hook, ch 18, join with a sl st to first ch to make a ring (image 7); ch 1, inc in each ch around; join with sl st to first sc. (36 sc) Join all rounds in this manner.

Round 2: Ch 1, sc in each st around; join. (36 sc)
At the end of Round 2, for the first Pants Leg, fasten off. For the second Pants Leg, do not fasten off.

Pants

Round 1: (*Joining Pants Legs*) Working on the first Pants Leg, sl st in last st made (image 8), ch 1, sc in each st around; working on the second Pants Leg, sc in each st around; join. (72 sc)

Rounds 2-12: (*11 Rounds*) Ch 1, sc in each st around; join. (72 sc)

Round 13: Ch 1, [sc-dec] 36 times; join. (36 sc)

Rounds 14-17: (*4 Rounds*) Ch 1, sc in each st around; join. (36 sc) At the end of Round 17, fasten off with invisible join.

Note: *If you would like to sew the Shorts to the Body, leave a long tail for sewing.*

Ruffle Detail

Working on Pants Leg, in the unused loops of foundation chain, attach Color C (image 9), [ch 3, sl st in next st] 18 times.

Fasten off and weave in ends. Repeat on other Pants Leg (image 10).

Mini Flower Appliqué
(Make 3 - one each of Color A, Pink & Blue)

Make a Magic Ring; ch 1, 5 sc in ring; tug tail to tighten ring; join with sl st to first sc. (5 sc) Fasten off, leaving a long tail for sewing (image 11).

» Sew the Flowers to front of Shorts (images 12, 13 & 14).

COLLAR

Row 1: (Right Side) Using Color C, ch 31, starting in the second ch from hook, sc in each ch across, change to Color B. (30 sc)

Row 2: Ch 3, turn, dc in each st across, change to Color A. (30 dc)

Row 3: (*Ruffle*) Turn, [ch 4, sl st in next st] 30 times. Fasten off and weave in ends.

Collar Ties

Using Color A, ch 20, with right side of Collar facing, working in unused loops of foundation chain (image 15), sc in each st across; ch 20. Fasten off (image 16).

FLOWERS

(image 17 - Big and Small Flowers)

Small Flower (Make 2 - one each in Color A & Blue)

Ch 8, starting in the third ch from hook, [3 dc in next ch, sc in next ch] 3 times. Fasten off, leaving a long tail.

» Shape the Flower, and using tail, sew to secure, leaving a tail for sewing (image 18).

Big Flower

Using Rose, ch 27, starting in the third ch from hook, [3 dc in next ch, sc in next ch] 5 times; change to Pink, [3 dc in each of next 2 ch, sc in next ch] 5 times. Fasten off, leaving a long tail.

» Roll the Flower into shape, and using tail, sew to secure, leaving a tail for sewing (image 19).

BUNNY ASSEMBLY (use photos as guide)

Eyes - Using Cotton Thread, embroider Sleeping Eyes between Rounds 15 & 16 of Head. The length of each Eye is 6 sts. The distance between the two Eyes is 6 sts (images 20, 21 & 22).

Nose - Using Old Rose, embroider a Nose between the Eyes (image 23).

Ears - Using long tail and yarn needle, fold the last round of Ear in half, and sew edges together (image 24). Repeat for other Ear. Position Ears on Head at Round 5 and sew in place (image 25).

Arms - Position the Arms on either side of the Body (2 rounds below the last round of Head). Using long tails and yarn needle, sew them in place.

Legs - Position the Legs on either side of the Body - 7 rounds from last round. Using long tails and yarn needle, sew them in place (image 26).

Flowers - Position and sew the Flowers on Head (image 27).

Face - Using a small makeup brush, apply blusher to the cheeks, and inside Ears (image 28).

Clothes - Pull on the Shorts, and tie the Collar around the neck (image 29).

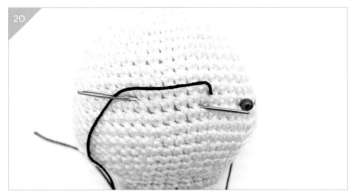

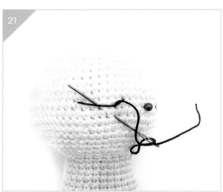

Willis The Goat

Spring has arrived and Willis is so happy! He loves prancing around the green fields, filling up his basket with lots of fresh and delicious grass.

MATERIALS

Scheepjes Softfun

Main Color (MC): White (2412)
Color A: Light Pink (2513)
Color B: Pink (2514)
Cream (2426) - small amount for Horns
Forest Green (2605) - small amount for Grasses

Scheepjes Softfun Denim

Brown (510) - small amount for Basket

Scheepjes Maxi Sweet Treat (Cotton Thread)

Black Coffee (162) - for Eyebrows

Size C-2 (2.75 mm) Crochet Hook - or size suitable for yarn used.
Yarn Needle
Embroidery Needle
Stitch Markers
⅜" (9 mm) Safety Eyes - 2
Toy Stuffing
Cosmetic Blusher & Brush - for Cheeks

Finished Size
About 7 ⅞" (20 cm) tall

Skill Level
♥

  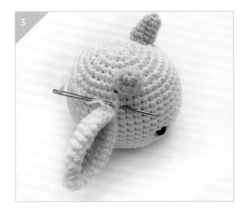

HEAD

Round 1: Using MC, make a Magic Ring; ch 1, 8 sc in ring, DO NOT JOIN. (8 sc) Tug tail to tighten ring. Mark last stitch.

Round 2: Inc in each st around. (16 sc) Move marker each round.

Round 3: [Sc in next st, inc in next st] 8 times. (24 sc)

Round 4: [Sc in each of next 2 sts, inc in next st] 8 times. (32 sc)

Round 5: Sc in next st, inc in next st, [sc in each of next 3 sts, inc in next st] 7 times, sc in each of next 2 sts. (40 sc)

Round 6: [Sc in each of next 4 sts, inc in next st] 8 times. (48 sc)

Rounds 7-10: *(4 Rounds)* Sc in each st around. (48 sc)

Round 11: [Sc in each of next 7 sts, inc in next st] 6 times. (54 sc)

Rounds 12-15: *(4 Rounds)* Sc in each st around. (54 sc)

Round 16: [Sc in each of next 8 sts, inc in next st] 6 times. (60 sc)

Round 17: Sc in each st around. (60 sc)

Round 18: [Sc in each of next 8 sts, **sc-dec**] 6 times. (54 sc)

Round 19: Sc in each of next 3 sts, sc-dec, [sc in each of next 7 sts, sc-dec] 5 times, sc in each of next 4 sts. (48 sc)

Round 20: [Sc in each of next 6 sts, sc-dec] 6 times. (42 sc)

Round 21: Sc in each of next 2 sts, sc-dec, [sc in each of next 5 sts, sc-dec] 5 times, sc in each of next 3 sts. (36 sc)

Round 22: [Sc in each of next 4 sts, sc-dec] 6 times. (30 sc)

Round 23: [Sc in each of next 3 sts, sc-dec] 6 times. (24 sc) Sl st in next st. Fasten off, leaving a long tail for sewing.

» Insert Safety Eyes between Rounds 15 & 16, about 9 stitches apart.

» Stuff Head firmly.

EAR (Make 2)

Note: *The colored font indicates where Color A is used. Use the Stranding Method for the color changes.*

Round 1: Using MC, make a Magic Ring; ch 1, 6 sc in ring, DO NOT JOIN. (6 sc) Tug tail to tighten ring. Mark last stitch.

Round 2: [Inc in next st, sc in next st] 3 times. (9 sc) Move marker each round.

Round 3: [Sc in each of next 2 sts, inc in next st] 3 times. (12 sc)

Round 4: [Inc in next st, sc in each of next 3 sts] 2 times; change to Color A, inc in next st; change to MC, sc in each of next 3 sts. (15 sc)

Round 5: Sc in next st, inc in next st, sc in each of next 4 sts, inc in next st, sc in each of next 3 sts; change to Color A, sc in next st, inc in next st; change to MC, sc in each of next 3 sts. (18 sc)

Round 6: Sc in each of next 2 sts, inc in next st, sc in each of next 5 sts, inc in next st, sc in each of next 3 sts; change to Color A, sc in each of next 2 sts, inc in next st; change to MC, sc in each of next 3 sts. (21 sc)

Rounds 7-10: *(4 Rounds)* Sc in each of next 14 sts; change to Color A, sc in each of next 4 sts; change to MC, sc in each of next 3 sts. (21 sc)

Round 11: [Sc-dec, sc in each of next 5 sts] 2 times; change to Color A, sc-dec, sc in each of next 2 sts; change to MC, sc in next of 3 sts. (18 sc)

Round 12: [Sc in next st, sc-dec] 4 times; change to Color A, sc in next st, sc-dec; change to MC, sc in next st, sc-dec. (12 sc) Fasten off Color A.

Last Row: Flatten the last round and working through both thicknesses, sc in each of next 6 sc. Fasten off, leaving a long tail for sewing.

HORN (Make 2)

Round 1: Using Cream, make a Magic Ring; ch 1, 6 sc in ring, DO NOT JOIN. (6 sc) Tug tail to tighten ring. Mark last stitch.

Round 2: [Inc in next st, sc in each of next 2 sts] 2 times. (8 sc) Move marker each round.

Round 3: Sc in each of next 7 sts, inc in the last st. (9 sc)

Round 4: Sc in each of next 8 sts, inc in the last st. (10 sc)

Round 5: Sc in each of next 9 sts, inc in the last st. (11 sc)

Round 6: Sc in each of next 10 sts, inc in the last st. (12 sc) Sl st in next st. Fasten off, leaving a long tail for sewing.

HEAD ASSEMBLY (use photos as guide)

Horns - Stuff Horns and position them on top of Head (between Rounds 4 & 6), and sew in place (image 1).

Ears - Using long tail and yarn needle, fold the last round of Ear in half, and sew sides together for 3 stitches (image 2). Repeat for other Ear. Position Ears on either side of Head (about 2 rounds under Horns) and sew in place (image 3).

 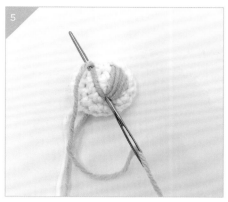 

Nose - Using Color A and yarn needle, embroider a Nose, one round below the Eyes (image 4).

Eyebrows - Using Cotton Thread and needle, embroider a straight stitch, 2 rounds above each Eye (image 4).

TAIL

Round 1: Using MC, make a Magic Ring; ch 1, 6 sc in ring, DO NOT JOIN. (6 sc) Tug tail to tighten ring. Mark last stitch.

Round 2: Inc in each st around. (12 sc) Move marker each round.

Round 3: [Sc in next st, inc in next st] 6 times. (18 sc)

Rounds 4-5: *(2 Rounds)* Sc in each st around. (18 sc)

Round 6: [Sc in next st, sc-dec] 6 times. (12 sc)

 » Stuff Tail lightly.

Round 7 [Sc in next st, sc-dec] 4 times. (8 sc) Sl st in next st. Fasten off, leaving a long tail for sewing.

 » Using Color A and yarn needle, embroider a heart on the Tail, using straight stitches (images 5 & 6).

ARM (Make 2)

Rounds 1-5: Using MC, repeat Rounds 1-5 of Tail. At the end of Round 5, there are 18 sc.

Round 6: [Sc in next st, sc-dec] 4 times, sc in each of next 6 sts. (14 sc)

Round 7: [Sc in each of next 2 sts, sc-dec] 2 times, sc in each of next 6 sts. (12 sc)

Round 8: Sc in each st around. (12 sc)

Round 9: [Sc in next st, sc-dec] 2 times, sc in each of next 6 sts. (10 sc)

Rounds 10-15: *(6 Rounds)* Sc in each st around. (10 sc)

 » Stuff Arm lightly.

Last Row: Flatten the last round and working through both thicknesses, sc in each of next 5 sc. Fasten off, leaving a long tail for sewing.

LEG (Make 2)

Rounds 1-2: Using Color B, repeat Rounds 1-2 of Tail. At the end of Round 2, there are 12 sc.

Round 3: [Sc in each of next 3 sts, inc in next st] around. (15 sc)

Round 4: Sc in each st around. (15 sc)
At the end of Round 4, change to MC. Fasten off Color B.

Rounds 5-8: *(4 Rounds)* Sc in each st around. (15 sc)
At the end of Round 8 - for the first Leg, fasten off. For the second Leg, do not fasten off.

BODY

Round 1: *(Joining Legs)* Start with the second Leg, ch 3; working on the first Leg, sc in last st made, sc in each of next 14 sts; working in ch-3, sc in each of next 3 ch; working on the second Leg, sc in each of next 15 sts; working in unused loops on the other side of ch-3, sc in each of next 3 ch. DO NOT JOIN (36 sc) Mark last st made. Move marker each round.

Round 2: [Sc in each of next 5 sts, inc in next st] 6 times. (42 sc)

Rounds 3-5: *(3 Rounds)* Sc in each st around. (42 sc)

Round 6: [Sc in each of next 5 sts, inc in next st] 7 times. (49 sc)

Rounds 7-10: *(4 Rounds)* Sc in each st around. (49 sc)

 » Start stuffing Legs and Body firmly, adding more as you go.

Round 11: [Sc in each of next 5 sts, sc-dec] 7 times. (42 sc)

Rounds 12-15: *(4 Rounds)* Sc in each st around. (42 sc)

Round 16: [Sc in each of next 5 sts, sc-dec] 6 times. (36 sc)

Rounds 17-19: *(3 Rounds)* Sc in each st around. (36 sc)

Round 20: [Sc in each of next 4 sts, sc-dec] 6 times. (30 sc)

Rounds 21-23: *(3 Rounds)* Sc in each st around. (30 sc)

Round 24: [Sc in each of next 3 sts, sc-dec] 6 times. (24 sc)

Rounds 25-27: *(3 Rounds)* Sc in each st around. (24 sc)
At the end of Round 35, change to Color B. Fasten off MC.

Round 28: *(Neck Frill)* With Color B, working in FLO, ch 3 *(counts as first dc)*, 3 dc in each st around; join with sl st to first dc. (72 dc) Fasten off and weave in ends.

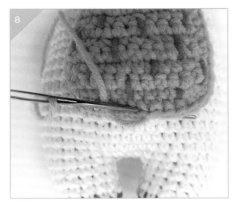

BELLY

Row 1: *(Right Side)* Using Color A, ch 13, starting in the second ch from hook, sc in each ch across. (12 sc)

Rows 2-4: *(3 rows)* Ch 1, turn, sc in each st across. (12 sc)

Row 5: Ch 1, turn, sc in each of next 3 sts, sc-dec, sc in each of next 2 sts, sc-dec, sc in each of next 3 sts. (10 sc)

Rows 6-8: *(3 rows)* Ch 1, turn, sc in each st across. (10 sc)

Row 9: Ch 1, turn, sc in each of next 4 sts, sc-dec, sc in each of next 4 sts. (9 sc)

Row 10: Ch 1, turn, sc in each st across. (9 sc)

Row 11: Ch 1, turn, sc in first st, hdc in each of next 2 sts, dc in next st, tr in next st, dc in next st, hdc in each of next 2 sts, sc in the last st. (9 sts)

Border Round: Ch 1, do not turn, evenly work sc around Belly; join with sl st to first sc.
Fasten off, leaving a long tail for sewing.

» Using Color B and yarn needle, embroider some small lines using straight stitches on the Belly (image 7).

BODY ASSEMBLY (use photos as guide)

Belly - Position and sew the Belly on the Body (image 8).

Arms - Position the Arms on either side of the Body about three rounds below Neck Frill. Using long tails and yarn needle, sew them in place (image 9).

Tail - Position and sew the Tail to center back of Body (image 10).

Head - Sew the Head to the Body, stuffing firmly before closing.

Face - Using a small makeup brush, apply blusher to the cheeks.

ACCESSORIES

Basket

Rounds 1-3: Using Brown, repeat Rounds 1-3 of Head. At the end of Round 3, there are 24 sc.

Rounds 4-7: *(4 Rounds)* Sc in each st around. (24 sc)

Round 8: [Sc in each of next 2 sts, sc-dec] 6 times. (18 sc)

Last Round: Sl st in each of next 9 sts; ch 51, starting in the second ch from hook, sl st in each ch across *(Basket Handle made)*; working in Round 8, sl st in each of next 9 sts.

Fasten off, leaving a long tail for sewing.

» Using the tail and yarn needle, sew the Handle to opposite side of Basket (image 11).

Grass (Make 5)

Using Forest Green, ch 15, starting in the second ch from hook, sc in each of next 4 ch; ch 5, starting in the second ch from hook, sc in each of next 4 ch; working in starting ch, sl st in each of remaining 10 ch. Fasten off and weave in ends (image 12).

» Place grass stalks in Basket.

ACKNOWLEDGEMENTS

To my dear little two-year old daughter, Anna, who is around me all day, every day – giving me all the happiness, energy and passion to discover this new world through her eyes. She is the reason I learnt to crochet, my endless inspiration, and a thousand things more than that. To my husband, my most patient supporter, who is always ready to listen a crazy idea, comment about my creations, and manage the whole household, giving me the free time in the evenings and weekends for me to complete this book. And to all my family and some close friends, for encouraging me along the way.

To Kader Demirpehlivan and the Tuva Publishing team, for the trust and the enormous support to help me make this dream come true.

To Wendi Cusins, for being so caring and patient with all my patterns (and my English!).

To the Scheepjes team, for the beautiful yarns you sent me - in the loveliest packaging.

And last but not least, to all of you, my dear crochet friends! Thank you for your crochet enthusiasm and your support. I wouldn't be able to do this job, nor to make this book project without you. Thank you for being with me on this amazing road of discovery. Even though we have never met in person, I feel we are so close, due to our shared passion.

From the bottom of my heart, thank you.

KHUC CAY